Pe

Autocrat and Reformer

By Michael W. Simmons

Copyright 2016 by Michael W. Simmons

Published by Make Profits Easy LLC

Profitsdaily123@aol.com

facebook.com/MakeProfitsEasy

Table of Contents

Chapter One: The Heir, the Regent, and the Tsars 4

Chapter Two: The Tsar in Europe 53

Chapter Three: The Great Northern War 99

Chapter Four: Poltava and Alexei 148

Chapter Five: The Legacy of Peter the Great ... 202

Further Reading 230

Chapter One: The Heir, the Regent, and the Tsars

The Russia of Alexei I

"I shall now give you a further description of the Czar. He is a goodly person, about six foot high, well set, inclined to fat, of a clear complexion, light hair, somewhat a low forehead, of a stern countenance, severe in his chastisements, but very careful of his Subjects love. Being urged by a Stranger to make it death for any man to desert his colors, he answered, it was a hard case to do that, for God has not given courage to all men alike. He never appears to the people but in magnificence, and on festivals with wonderful splendor of jewels and attendants. He never went to any subject's house but his governor's when he was thought past all recovery. His sentinels and guards, placed round about his court, stand like silent and immoveable statues. No noise is heard in his palace, no more than if uninhabited. None but his domestics are suffered to approach the inward Court, except the lords that are in office. He never dines publicly but on festivals, and then his nobility dine in his presence. At Easter all the nobility and gentry, and Courtiers kiss the emperor's hand, and receive eggs. Every meal he sends dishes of meat to his favorites from his own table. His stores of corn, and dried flesh are very considerable, with these he pays his Streltsy or Janissaries, giving them some cloth, but very little money; for they have all trades, and great privileges...

'Tis death for anyone to reveal what is spoken in the palace. I being curious to see the fine buildings for the flax and hemp, asked to what end they were built, but not a workman durst tell me, though they know it well enough; but they replied, God and the Emperor know best, this was all I could get from them. The

Czars' children are attended with children of their own bred up with them, and there is none of them but know their distance, and their degrees of bowing to all sorts of persons. None dare speak a word what passes in their Court."

> Samuel Collins, personal physician to Tsar Alexei I, 1660-1670

The Romanov dynasty had existed for less than sixty years when Peter the Great was born on June 9, 1672. In 1613, his grandfather, the sixteen-year-old Michael Romanov, had been offered the bankrupt, moth-eaten throne of the tsars after over a decade of chaos and civil war, known as the Time of Troubles, during which there had been no supreme ruler in Russia. Sickly, unprepared, lacking in allies, Michael had nonetheless managed to prepare his son Alexei superbly for the position he would inherit. Alexei I was well-educated for a Russian of his era, reform-minded, strictly religious, and beloved by his subjects. To peasant and noble alike, the tsar was father of his people, "batushka", and his authority over them was supreme, as the authority of a father over his children was supreme. Alexei had a reputation for piety besides; he was called "the Young Monk" during the early years of his reign, and even priests of the Russian Orthodox church who visited the tsar's court found it a challenge to keep up with his daily schedule of prayers and masses, which began before dawn and continued throughout the day.

Alexei's first wife was Maria Miloslavsky, a girl four years his senior whom the tsar had selected out of a final group of six contestants in a traditional brideshow, a sort of beauty contestant for the daughters of the minor nobility. The winner of the brideshow became tsarina and her family were elevated to a place of honor and influence in the tsar's court. Alexei's union with

Miloslavsky produced thirteen children. She died in 1669, after twenty-one years of marriage, due to complications from her fourteenth pregnancy. Despite the birth of so many children, only a few of them had survived infancy, and only two of them were boys. Of these two potential heirs, the elder, Fyodor, was sickly, and the younger, Ivan, was partially blind and considered to be "slow"—what sort of disability or impairment he had is uncertain, but it was plain that he could never rule Russia alone. Alexei decided to marry again, in the hopes of producing more sons.

The girl of nineteen whom Alexei chose as his next tsarina was remarkable, even unique, amongst the young Russian women of her day. Her name was Natalya Naryshkina, and she was the ward of Arteem Matveev and his wife Mary Hamilton, a Scottish refugee from Cromwell's anti-royalist regime. Matveev and Hamilton lived in the German Quarter, the only area of Moscow where foreigners were permitted to reside, and they hosted regular salons where the science, art, literature, and technology of the west were celebrated. Alexei was a regular visitor to their home; unlike most Russians, he had studied western languages as a boy, and he took an interest in the lives of the foreigners dwelling in his city.

In the late 17th century, people at even the highest levels of Russian society were unaware and uncaring of the amusements or advancements that enlivened the existence of their European counterparts. Russia, though massive, was landlocked for most of the year when its sole port city, Archangel, was frozen over. The nations that bordered Russia, particularly Sweden and Austria, took care to keep their neighbor isolated, by checking any attempt to gain control of southern waterways in the Baltic. But Russia's isolation was cultural and religious as well as geographical. The Orthodox church held no communion with Roman

Catholicism; Russians looked east to Kiev, to Constantinople, for its religious and cultural near neighbors. Russian men wore long beards as a sign of their devotion to God, not unlike Muslim men; noble Russian women lived in the *terem*, on the upper floors of their family home, entirely segregated from the lives of the men. In public they veiled their faces and at church or at court functions they remained behind grilled partitions. As historian Robert Massie puts it,

"The higher a lady's rank and the more gorgeous her wardrobe, the less likely she was to be seen. The Muscovite idea of women, derived from Byzantium, had nothing of those romantic medieval Western conceptions of gallantry, chivalry, and the Court of Love. Instead, a woman was regarded as a silly, helpless child, intellectually void, morally irresponsible, and, given the slightest chance, enthusiastically promiscuous. This puritanical idea that an element of evil lurked in all little girls affected their earliest childhood. In good families, children of opposite sexes were never allowed to play together—to preserve the boys from contamination. As they grew older, girls, too, were subject to contamination, and even the most innocent contact between youths and maidens were forbidden. Instead, to preserve their purity while teaching them prayer, obedience and a few useful skills such as embroidery, daughters were kept under lock and key. A song described them as 'sitting behind thirty locked doors, so that the wind may not ruffle their hair, nor the sun burn their cheeks, nor the handsome young men entice them.' Thus they waited, ignorant and undefiled, until the day came to thrust them into the hands of a husband."

In stark contrast to such traditions, Mary Hamilton played hostess to her husband's male visitors in the European style, guiding conversations, serving refreshments, arranging for entertainment—in short, being anything other than cloistered and invisible. At her side sat Natalya Naryshkina, learning social graces she could scarcely have learned anywhere else in Russia. Alexei met Naryshkina during a visit to Matveev's house; she served him vodka, he engaged her in conversation, and was reportedly impressed by the modesty and cleverness blended in her responses. It was the first time he had ever encountered a young Russian woman outside his own family in a social setting, so it is scarcely to be wondered that she made a significant impression on him. Alexei asked Matveev what arrangements had been made for the young woman's future. Matveev explained that she was very popular with the men who visited his home, but no one had offered to marry her, due to the fact that neither he nor her father could offer much in the way of a dowry. Alexei told Matveev that he knew of a man who loved her, and had no need of a dowry, and that he, Alexei, could arrange the match if Naryshkina was willing. Matveev replied that, though Naryshkina would undoubtedly be delighted to consent to a match arranged for her by the tsar himself, she would probably wish to know the man's name before she gave her consent. Alexei agreed that this was reasonable, and told Matveev that it was he who wished to marry her.

Alexei's declaration was nothing less than earthshaking, both to the Matveev household and the entire Russian court. In Europe, intermarriage between the royal houses of different countries were arranged to secure alliances. In isolated Russia, however, the tsar could only marry an Orthodox bride, partly for religious reasons, partly because European families were unwilling to send their daughters on a long, dangerous journey to a country that was considered primitive, even savage. The tsar's marriage, therefore, defined the balance of power in the Russian court. For as long as the tsar lived and the marriage prospered, the tsarina's family enjoyed a position of power and influence second only to the Romanovs themselves. But a Russian royal marriage could be ended with considerably less trouble than a European one. Henry VIII had to defy a pope and establish a new religion with himself as its head in order to divorce his first wife, Katherine of Aragon. The Russian tsar had only to send his tsarina to a convent to become a nun, and the marriage became void, his remarriage cleared of legal obstacles. If the tsarina fell out of favor, by failing to produce a son or for any other reason, not only she, but her entire family, stood to lose everything, even their lives.

There was neither check nor balance against the tsar's power. He was the supreme autocrat, and his word was law. By choosing Matveev's ward as his bride, Alexei was elevating Matveev, who was not from a high ranking noble family, to dizzying heights; but if Naryshkina should prove a disappointment, Matveev might just as easily find himself executed or exiled. And it was not only the tsar's displeasure that Matveev and Naryshkina had to fear. The family of the widowed Alexei's first tsarina, the Miloslavskys, would jealously guard their power in the court against the faction that would form around the new tsarina. The Miloslavskys could not prevent Matveev and the Naryshkins from gaining preeminence, but as family to the young princes Fyodor and Ivan, they could not be set aside either. The rivalry between the families of the two tsarinas would define Russian politics for the next twenty years.

At Matveev's insistence, Natalya Naryshkina went through the formality of participating in a brideshow, during which the Miloslavskys accused Matveev of using witchcraft to ensnare the tsar's affections. Nonetheless, the marriage took place on February 1, 1671. The western influences in Naryshkina's upbringing marked the beginning of the end of Russia's strict adherence to old Muscovite traditions and complete isolation from Europe. When her son Peter became tsar, he would order his courtiers to cut their long Orthodox beards; in 1671, Natalya upset the court nearly as much by going out in public in a carriage without heavy curtains to screen her from view. She sat next to the tsar at state functions, instead of keeping behind the women's partition. Music and dancing had long been forbidden by the strictly pious Alexei, but because Natalya had learned to love music under Mary Hamilton's tutelage, music and dancing were introduced at court. To most Russians, these changes were very welcome. But Natalya was already making enemies, among them Alexei's daughters by Maria Miloslavsky, some of whom were older than their nineteen-year-old stepmother. The most intelligent of the sisters, Sophia Alekseyevna, thirteen at the time of the marriage, hated Natalya most of all.

Natalya and Alexei's son Peter was born in June of 1672 (May 30 in the Gregorian calendar.) By the age of two he had his own apartments in the Kremlin, overflowing with toys. His favorite plaything was a model ship given to him by Matveev; Peter's interest in shipbuilding would last throughout his life, and eventually lead to the establishment of a Russian navy. Tsar Alexei doted on his wife and young son, taking the intelligent, energetic toddler with him to greet the public and meet foreign ministers. But five years after Alexei and Natalya were married, when Peter was a little more than three years old, Alexei died of a sudden illness. With his father's passing came a complete change in Peter's status. He was no longer the son of the living tsar but the half-brother of the sickly new tsar Fyodor III. Though Alexei had recently declared the fifteen-year-old Fyodor to be of age and officially recognized him as his heir, it was taken as little more than a gesture of paternal affection; Fyodor, it was thought, would undoubtedly predecease his robust father, who would then recognize his youngest son Peter as his successor. With Alexei gone, however, and the son of Maria Miloslavsky on the Russian throne, the Naryshkins were out of favor. Fyodor was fond of his youngest brother and of his stepmother, but he could not prevent his relatives from confining Natalya and Peter to a country estate, far away from the seat of political power.

The death of Tsar Fyodor

Educational standards in Russia during Peter's childhood were less than rigorous, compared to the sort of education that a young European prince was expected to attain. It was not uncommon for nobles to be as illiterate as peasants. Tsar Fyodor and his sister Sophia were exceptions; both had received classical educations at the hands of theological tutors and could speak Latin and Polish, Polish having the same utility to a Russian noble that French had to a European one. The tutor assigned to oversee Peter's education had none of these qualifications; he was chosen chiefly because of his profound knowledge of Scripture. Natalya Naryshkina was only concerned that Peter learn to read and write, but though Peter was a restless student, he was eager to expand his knowledge of geography and Russian history. Knowledge of these fields stood him in excellent stead when he became the first tsar of Russia to travel outside of his homeland.

Fyodor lived and reigned for six years after Alexei's death. He married twice, but neither marriage produced sons. When he died in 1682, the succession was unclear for the first time in the history of the Romanov dynasty, which had transferred power seamlessly from father to son for three generations.

Fyodor's brother Ivan would be his natural successor, except that everyone knew Ivan was mentally unfit to rule. His Miloslavsky relatives, eager to seize power through a regency on Ivan's behalf, pressed his claim. Fyodor and Ivan's half-brother, Peter, was already tall and strong, active and intelligent, but he was only ten years old and the Miloslavskys were unwilling to accept a Naryshkin regent. Both the Miloslavskys and Naryshkins would have to be satisfied before a decision could be made, but they were incapable of coming to an agreement. During an assembly of boyars, the cry went up that "the people" should decide which boy would be tsar, so Patriarch Joachim of the Orthodox church guided both Peter and Ivan onto a balcony and presented them to the crowds gathered below the palace, asking them to choose their tsar. The sound of Peter's name being shouted quickly drowned out the sound of Ivan's.

The Streltsy Revolt

The Miloslavskys were predictably disheartened by Peter's acclamation and the return of the Naryshkin faction to power, none more so than the twenty-five-year-old tsarevna Sophia. As the daughter and sister of tsars, Sophia ought to have lived her entire life in the *terem* apartments in the uppermost floors of the Kremlin, leaving home only to attend church and go on pilgrimage, when she would be hidden from the world by the veils she wore and the curtains on the windows. But somehow she defied this destiny. We do not know why tsar Alexei chose to permit Sophia, out of all his daughters, to attend lessons with her brother, the future tsar Fyodor, but he did, and her education was accordingly excellent. She was the third oldest of Alexei's eight daughters, one of twelve female inmates of the terem. Nothing distinguished her except her own exceptional qualities. She was a capable student, praised by her tutors as "a maiden of great intelligence" and superior understanding. During Fyodor's reign, while her Miloslavsky relatives held power in the court, Sophia began to expand the boundaries of her world even further, attending council sessions, conversing with male politicians, comparing her intellectual powers with those of the men who ran the Russian court.

By the time tsar Fyodor died, Sophia had matured in confidence and had amassed more influence than anyone realized. She was accustomed to the freedom of life outside the terem. When her half-brother Peter was elected tsar by public acclamation, Sophia was savvy enough to understand that she would probably be sent back in the terem, not only because her Miloslavsky relatives would be replaced at court by the Naryshkins, but because Natalya Naryshkina would be regent, and she and Sophia had always been at odds with one another. Demonstrating just how politically astute she had become, Sophia began her campaign to alter the balance of power in her favor at her brother's funeral. During Fyodor's funeral procession, she stepped out of her veiled canopy—another shocking departure from custom—and displayed her wailing and weeping to the public, underscoring the fact that the dead tsar was her dearly beloved brother. Natalya Naryshkina retaliated by taking the ten-year-old Peter home from the funeral service early, claiming that he was too tired and hungry to endure the whole service. This proved to be a severe miscalculation; in the absence of the new tsar and the regent, all eyes were on the bereaved tsarevna, who loudly, theatrically, bemoaned her orphaned state, proclaimed that her brother Fyodor had been poisoned by the Naryshkins, and insinuated that a similar fate awaited her young brother Ivan.

Sophia's public accusations soon triggered a revolt amongst the Streltsy, an enormous division of soldiers armed with muskets and pikes created by Ivan the Terrible to guard the tsar in the Kremlin. Numbering 20,000, they were the heart of the Russian army. Most of the Streltsy were unlettered, unsophisticated peasants, under the charge of noble officers. At the time of tsar Fyodor's death, the Streltsy were already in a state of unrest; their pay was being embezzled by their officers, and when one soldier made an official complaint on behalf of the whole regiment, the Streltsy commander ordered that he be beaten for insubordination. This incited a total of seventeen Streltsy regiments to rebel against their officers, and the rebellion was still ongoing when Natalya Naryshkina took office as regent. The Streltsy were so numerous that they occupied an entire quarter of the city of Moscow; their demands could not be ignored when they acted together. Natalya attempted to placate them by having their colonels arrested and their property confiscated to pay the soldiers their wages. But the Streltsy had already made a connection between the unfair treatment they had received and the accusations Sophia had made against the Naryshkins. They smelled a conspiracy; in order to preserve the live of the tsarevitch Ivan, he must be placed on the throne and the Naryshkin faction purged. They were encouraged in this belief by high ranking members of the Miloslavsky faction, who were probably conspiring with Sophia herself. But it would be difficult to overthrow Peter and replace him with Ivan unless another member of the royal family stood ready to step into Natalya Naryshkina's place as regent. Sophia, however, possessed the necessary intelligence and daring, and most importantly of all, as tsar Alexei's daughter, she possessed legitimacy. Without her, the plot to place Ivan on the throne could not have succeeded.

On May 15, 1682, two members of the Miloslavsky faction appeared in the midst of the Streltsy and claimed that the Naryshkins had killed Ivan and were planning to kill Sophia and all the rest of tsar Alexei's children. Only the faithful soldiers of the Streltsy could prevent the murders of a dozen Romanovs, most of whom were women and children. At once, the Streltsy began to march on the Kremlin. Panic and confusion ensued; the soldiers were within the walls of the fortress and inside the palace itself before any defense could be mounted against them. Natalya Naryshkina, learning that the Streltsy believed Ivan to be dead, took both Ivan and Peter by the hands and led them to the top of the grand staircase, where the Streltsy were gathered. "Thanks be to God they are well and have not suffered at the hands of traitors," she told them. "There are no traitors in the palace. You have been deceived."

At first it seemed that the tide had been turned and violence would be averted. Arteem Matveev, Natalya Naryshkina's former guardian, her chief advisor now that she was regent, promised the Streltsy that their actions would be forgiven if they dispersed immediately, since they had acted out of loyalty to the tsar. The soldiers were on the verge of obeying him when Prince Michael Dolgoruky—son of the very commanding officer who had allowed their colonels to embezzle their wages—began to berate them, threatening mass punishments. Instantly, their rage against the nobles and the Naryshkins was rekindled, and slaughter ensued. Dolgoruky and Matveev were both impaled, thrown from the balcony onto the pikes of the soldiers below. Matveev was dragged away before the eyes of Natalya, Peter, and Ivan, and hacked to pieces. The Streltsy went from room to room throughout the Kremlin, hunting for Natalya's male Naryshkin relatives, forcing servants and passers-by to assist them in their search at sword point.

No one attempted to harm Peter, Ivan, or Natalya, but all three were forced to stand in the midst of the carnage and watch as the Streltsy went on their rampage, hacking and impaling

Peter and Natalya's family with abandon. Throughout the ordeal, ten-year-old Peter remained silent and watchful, betraying none of the horror he must have felt. But the traumatic effects of witnessing the Streltsy revolt remained with him for the rest of his life; some scholars have speculated that it was the source of the epileptic fits he suffered as an adult. The revolt lasted for three days, with the soldiers returning to their own homes at night and coming back to the palace in the morning on the hunt for more of the "traitors" who had supposedly murdered tsar Fyodor. When the dust settled at last, the Streltsy were very nearly de facto rulers of Moscow; the boyars and royals dared refuse none of their demands. Ivan was named co-tsar with Peter at their petition, and their sister Sophia was likewise appointed regent. Sophia, who undoubtedly played some role in instigating the revolt but probably had not anticipated the full consequences, was in fact the candidate best-suited to rule among those who had survived the violence. She was careful to reward the Streltsy in accordance with their idea of themselves as faithful protectors of the tsar and his government.

Peter, meanwhile, was irrevocably marked by the violence he had witnessed. It would not be overstating matters to describe the Streltsy revolt as the defining event of his formative years. The entire course of his adolescence and young adulthood can be mapped with respect to the brutal realities Peter learned while watching a poorly organized, poorly led force of traditional Muscovite soldiers slaughter his family before his eyes. One historian describes the effects of the Streltsy revolt upon Peter thus:

"Peter hated what he had seen: the maddened, undisciplined soldiery of the old medieval Russia running wild through the Kremlin; statesmen and nobles dragged from their private chambers and bloodily massacred;

Moscow, the Kremlin, the royal family, the Tsar himself at the mercy of ignorant, rioting soldiers. The revolt helped create in Peter a revulsion against the Kremlin, with its dark rooms and mazes of tiny apartments lit by flickering candles, its population of bearded priests and boyars, its pathetically secluded women. He extended his hatred to Moscow, the capital of the Orthodox tsars, and to the Orthodox Church, with its chanting priests, pomp and ceremony which could call him 'next to God' but could not protect him or his mother when the Streltsy turned against them."

Peter would spend his adolescence distancing himself as much as possible from the trappings of old Muscovy. For friendship, entertainment, adventure, and romance, he turned to Moscow's German quarter, where he mingled with foreigners and other disreputables, shunning the trappings and ceremonies of royalty. When Peter came into his maturity, his fascination with the society, technologies, and military traditions of Europe would lead him on a journey west; when he returned to Russia, it was at the head of a cultural revolution. And Moscow itself would be shunned by the tsar in his adulthood, as his vision swung towards the Baltic, where he would build the city of St. Petersburg, a new capital for a new Russia.

The Regency of Sophia Alekseyevna

Tsarevna Sophia Alekseyevna became, at the age of twenty-five, the first woman ever to rule Russia—first in a string of female regents and empresses that would dominate the late 17th and 18th centuries. Indeed, Peter the Great was the only significant male monarch to rule Russia until after the death of Catherine the Great more than a hundred years later.

Those who had conspired to help Sophia become regent were not necessarily eager to make the experiment in female rule, however. Prince Ivan Khovansky, one of the Streltsy commanders who had stirred the soldiers up against the Naryshkins, saw Sophia's regency as a necessary but troublesome obstacle on the path towards making *himself* regent. Khovansky was an Old Believer, one of those who had held out against the religious reforms implemented by tsar Alexei to make the doctrines and practices of the Russian Orthodox church consistent with the Greek Orthodox rite. A large number of the Streltsy were also Old Believers. Testing his influence over the new regent, Khovansky presented Sophia with the Streltsy's demand that she overturn Alexei's religious reforms. He had good reason to believe that this demand would be honored; the Streltsy received practically everything they asked for in the wake of the revolt, including a monument in Red Square honoring their deeds and listing the names of their victims as traitors to be reviled for all of history. Cannily, Sophia promised Khovansky that she would do all that he asked—just as soon as she had discharged her duty in arranging the double coronation of her brothers Ivan and Peter. In Europe, it sometimes happened that husbands and wives were crowned co-rulers, but this was to be the first time in the history of Russia or Europe that two brothers would share the throne of a nation. The coronation took place quickly, within a week of Sophia's becoming regent.

As it happened, Sophia had no intention of overturning her father's church reforms. In July of 1682, she and the other women of the royal family—including her own sisters, tsar Fyodor's wife Martha, and Peter's mother Natalya—walked out to meet a mob of Streltsy Old Believers who had come to see their demands fulfilled. Embodying the peremptory spirit of a true Romanov autocrat, Sophia informed them that to reverse her father's religious edicts would be to call into question the authority the tsar who had decreed them. Khovansky hinted that it was past time for Sophia to retreat to a convent. Sophia responded by executing huge numbers of the Streltsy for their role in the Moscow rebellion. She spared Khovansky in order to test his loyalty, by giving him charge of the government in her absence while she took Ivan and Peter on pilgrimage. There, miles from the palace, she wrote to Khovansky, requesting that he send a large number of the palace guard to meet the young tsars and accompany them on their journey. Khovansky was unwilling to surrender the men and arms under his command, and Sophia took this as evidence that he was planning to mount a coup. She had Khovansky arrested, condemned as a traitor, and publicly executed. No one would suggest that she retreat to a convent again until her brother Peter sent her there seven years later.

Two years into her regency, in 1684, Sophia was at war. The Ottoman empire had attacked Vienna; Russia joined with other Christian nations, including its hereditary enemy, Catholic Poland, to fight for Christendom. In exchange, Russia would receive rights over Kiev, the historical birthplace of Russian Orthodox Christianity, as well as much of Ukraine. Though Sophia made the decisions, she involved the young tsars in the diplomatic negotiations. Eighteen-year-old Ivan was halting, awkward, participating only when prompted; by contrast, Peter, who was twelve, listened carefully to the ambassadors and asked so many questions that he had to be reminded that as a matter of protocol he was supposed to let Ivan speak first. He had proven too restless to spend long hours in a traditional classroom as he grew older, but he was already eager to exert his authority.

Peter's education

In a way, the decline in the political fortunes of the Naryshkin faction served Peter exceptionally well in his boyhood. As regent, Sophia kept Natalya Naryshkina on an allowance too small to permit any extravagance, so she and Peter lived in the village of Preobrazhenskoe, about three miles outside of Moscow, where Peter grew up in the fresh air, forests, and streams of the countryside. The royal tutors who had provided tsar Alexei's other children with a classical education were far away in the Kremlin, so Peter's formal studies fell by the wayside. He was anything but idle, however. Peter was the first in a long line of Romanov tsars who were military-mad as children. Like most royal children, his first friends were assigned to him from amongst the sons of the most powerful families at court, boys his age whose fathers were high-ranking boyars. To this core group of six or seven boys, Peter added dozens, and eventually hundreds of new recruits from every class of society, including boys whose fathers were merchants, servants, or serfs. He organized these followers into a "play" regiment, the Preobrazhensky Guards—though their "play" status was due only to the age of most of the participants. In almost every particular, they were outfitted and disciplined in the style of a legitimate military regiment. They lived in barracks, adhered to a strict schedule of sentry duty, wore uniforms, and drilled with real weapons. Peter requisitioned cannon and gunpowder so that he could practice firing salutes. No doubt many children have dreamed of playing war games with such toys, but Peter was tsar, and Sophia Alekseyevna allowed the requisitions to be granted, in deference to his status. There was no reason for her to deny his requests. Peter was still too young to be any threat to her, and even if he and all his boy soldiers had marched on the Kremlin, her regency was supported by the Streltsy in Moscow.

Over time, nearly the entire Preobrazhenskoe village was caught up in Peter's military games and the nearby village of Semyonovksoe was annexed as well, leading to the creation of the Semyonovsky Guards. Once Peter became tsar in his own right, the Preobrazhensky and Semyonovsky would become the first two regiments in the Russian Imperial Guard; they would play crucial roles in bringing the future empresses Elizaveta and Catherine the Great to the throne, and they would endure until the fall of the Russian monarchy in 1917. After Peter, the rank of colonel of the Preobrazhensky Guards belonged to the tsar by right, but Peter himself insisted on starting at the bottom ranks of his play army, as a drummer boy, only allowing himself to be promoted when he felt that his experience and abilities were suited to a higher rank. This was partly because drummer boys have more fun than the boy playing the rank of colonel, but even when Peter was older he rarely took supreme command of his armies, though he was always present when the most dangerous battles were fought. Peter's reign was distinguished by his insistence on merit-based promotions; in this, he often upset the boyars, who were accustomed to the privileges of precedence and did not like to take orders from anyone who was socially beneath them. But it became difficult for a boyar officer to argue when the son of a merchant was promoted over his head, when the tsar himself was abiding by the same standards.

Peter was anxious that his play regiments have professional instruction from real soldiers and officers. These, he recruited from Moscow's German suburb. Peter was fascinated by the military tactics practiced by European armies, and these foreign-born soldiers of fortune who had washed up in Moscow's foreign quarter were well-equipped to teach him. Peter looked for other teachers as well—before the age of fifteen, he learned carpentry, stonemasonry, printing, blacksmithing, and how to operate a wood-lathe. Then, in 1687, he met a Dutch merchant named Franz Timmerman, who, at Peter's request, introduced the young tsar to the art of shipbuilding. As the story goes, Peter and Timmerman were out walking one day when they came across a storehouse that had been locked for twenty years. Peter asked to look inside, where he discovered the decaying remains of what Timmerman identified as "an English boat". It was like no boat Peter had ever seen before. Russian riverboats were similar to barges and had to be pushed along by the wind, the current, or by people manning oars or simply hauling the boat downriver with rope. Russia had only one seaport, and therefore Russia had no navy and no merchant fleet. Peter had never seen or even heard of a ship that was designed to sail against the wind in oceanic waters. He asked Timmerman whether the boat could be repaired, and Timmerman agreed to undertake the project. Once the boat was seaworthy again,

Peter was on the water daily. Shipbuilding became his new passion. He spent much of 1687 building a boatyard on the shores of Lake Pleschev, where a crew of Dutch shipbuilders began construction on two frigates and three yachts.

It was with great unwillingness that Peter left this project behind in 1688, returning to Moscow on orders from his mother. He was sixteen years old; it was time, both his mother and his sister Sophia agreed, for Peter to be married. Natalya Naryshkina disapproved of all the time Peter was spending in the company of foreigners. She handpicked his bride, believing that a sweet, pretty, obedient girl from a traditional family would be just the thing to capture her son's attention and anchor him back in Moscow, where the political climate was becoming unstable. Peter obeyed his mother's summons and went through with the wedding, but it was a disaster from day one. His wife, Eudoxia

Lopukhina, had been cloistered in a terem her whole life and had no education at all. She was everything a traditional Muscovite bride was supposed to be, painfully deferential, obedient, over-awed by her husband, but Peter was bored senseless by her. They had two sons. The elder, Alexei, became his heir. The younger, Alexander, died as an infant. Peter was by that time so detached from his wife and his domestic ties that he did not bother attending the child's funeral.

End of the regency

At sixteen, Peter was the same age that his father, tsar Alexei, and his grandfather, the first Romanov tsar, Michael, had been when they came to the throne. He had long since reached his adult height of six feet, eight inches. (Visiting Swedish ministers, meeting the strapping Peter when he was eleven years old, reported home that he was at least sixteen, so impressive did he appear physically.) By comparison, his brother and co-tsar Ivan was weak, shy, and found it distressing when he was required to make decisions.

The first few years of Sophia Alekseyevna's regency had been successful, even peaceful. She had successfully negotiated to retain Russian rights over Kiev in exchange for fighting alongside the Polish against the Ottoman empire; this was the greatest triumph of her reign. But by the late 1680's, Russia was embroiled, through treaty agreements with Poland, in a war against the Crimean Tatars. At the head of this campaign was Sophia's foreign minister, chief advisor, and lover, Vasily Golitsyn. Russian forces met with heavy losses, and Golitsyn was forced to retreat on unfavorable terms; the Khan of Crimea refused to release Russian prisoners, or cease his attacks against Ukraine and Poland. Nonetheless,

Sophia greeted Golitsyn as a hero at the gates of Moscow and ordered thanksgiving services to be held in the city's churches. In the names of tsar Ivan and tsar Peter, she lavished Golitsyn with rewards in the form of money and a country estate. Peter, however, refused his consent for these honors. He refused to attend the thanksgiving services for Golitsyn's return, and when Golitsyn traveled to Peter's home in the country to offer formal thanks for the rewards Sophia had dispensed in Peter's name, Peter refused to see him. "Everyone saw plainly and knew that the consent of the younger Tsar had not been extorted without the greatest difficulty and that this merely made him more excited against the generalissimo," wrote Patrick Gordon, a Scottish soldier who had advised Sophia during her preparations for war.

This was the first time Peter had publically challenged Sophia's authority as regent. He was old enough by now that such behavior could not be seen as anything but an opening gambit in a campaign to end the regency. The Russian court, sensing that a shift in power was rapidly approaching, began to pay greater attention to the young tsar and his mother at their estate in Preobrazhenskoe. The atmosphere was tense. Unconfirmed rumors were circulating that Sophia intended to have herself crowned as tsarina, setting her brothers aside, after which she would marry Golitsyn and make him tsar. There was no evidence that she was planning such a move, save that a portrait had been painted of her wearing the traditional regalia of Russian autocrats, including the cap of Monomakh, with which all tsars of Russia were crowned. But it is certain that, having tasted the freedom, power, and independence of being regent, she was fearful of being relegated to terem life once again. If she suspected the fate that awaited her after Peter gained his majority, perhaps she would have done something to deserve the charges that were being leveled against her.

In June of 1689, tensions erupted between Sophia and the Miloslavsky faction in the Kremlin and Peter, Natalya, and the Naryshkins in Preobrazhenskoe. Peter was beginning to resent Sophia's customary practice of appearing in royal processions on equal footing with her brothers; Sophia, feeling that she was only exercising the rights bestowed upon her at her brothers' coronation, refused to take a lower place. Neither Peter nor Sophia could launch an open attack against the other without a good reason. Sophia was afraid that Peter would send the Preobrazhensky and Semyonovsky regiments to attack her. Peter, having witnessed the savagery of the Streltsy attack against his relatives as a boy, worried that if Sophia ordered them to attack him, they would obey. In August of that year, Peter's worst fears seemed to be confirmed when Streltsy guards attacked a messenger Peter had sent to the Kremlin. When Peter's retainers heard of it, they woke him in the middle of the night, telling him that the Streltsy were coming to murder him; such was his terror that he fled forty-five miles on horseback to reach his supporters who were gathered at the fortified Troitsky Monastery. There was no need for such panicked flight; Sophia had not ordered any attack against Peter. But it was difficult to explain what had really happened, and in any case, Peter had decided that he was no longer content to be ruled by a regent.

At Troitsky Monastery, Peter was not only surrounded by his own supporters, but by the walls of an impregnable fortress, which also happened to be one of the holiest sites in Russia. Even if the Streltsy attacked, they could not reach him there. But the Streltsy were not likely to launch such an attack. They were conservative, traditional, and blindly loyal to the tsar. Lacking anything like political sophistication, they were uncertain how to choose between the duly appointed regent

Sophia and the anointed sovereign tsar Ivan on the one side, and the anointed sovereign tsar Peter on the other. Peter decided to test his authority and find out which way the Streltsy would fall by ordering Ivan Tsykler, colonel of the Stremyani Regiment, to join him at Troitsky, along with fifty of his men. Once Tsykler was actually in Peter's presence, he became obedient and humble, promising to do whatever Peter wished, so long as he would protect them against any reprisals from his sister. Peter then wrote to the colonels of all the other Streltsy regiments, ordering them to leave the Kremlin and come to Troitsky, but they were as overwhelmed by Sophia's proximity as Tsykler had been by Peter's—she threatened to behead any of the Streltsy that tried to leave Moscow, and the colonels, at least, listened to her. Day by day, ordinary soldiers were deserting their posts near the Kremlin to travel to Preobrazhenskoe and present themselves as faithful subjects of the younger tsar.

Sophia did not wish to attack, depose, imprison, or kill Peter; throughout the summer, she attempted to reconcile with him. But reconciliation meant that Peter would remain under Sophia's authority, something he was no longer willing to do. In truth, once Peter realized that his greatest strength lay in the legitimacy of his position as tsar, there was nothing Sophia could do to stop him from taking power.

Since neither Sophia nor Peter was willing to fight, everything depended on the loyalty of the Streltsy and foreign officers in Moscow, like Patrick Gordon, who held key positions in the Russian army. The Streltsy, though they were 20,000 strong and capable of terrible destruction, were almost childlike in their deference to whoever they perceived as having rightful authority over them. The trouble lay in controlling this perception, because they were liable to being influenced. Peter, it turned out, was enormously influential. And many of the foreign officers had helped train Peter's play regiments when he was a boy. They knew his character well enough to understand which way the wind was blowing.

On August 4, 1689, Peter sent a message to the Kremlin declaring that Fyodor Shaklovity, Sophia's chief lieutenant besides Golitsyn, had conspired against his life; he ordered that Shaklovity be arrested and sent to Troitsky to face justice. The news came as a shattering blow to Sophia. The Streltsy remaining in Moscow had come to realize that they were now on the losing side of the power contest between the regent and the tsar, and they demanded that she turn Shaklovity over to them so that they might take him to Troitsky as a sign of their obedience. Sophia refused, until they threatened to rise up against her, storming the Kremlin as they had done seven years ago in their purge of the Naryshkins. The Streltsy had brought her to power, and now they would bring her low again. One by one, Peter ordered the arrest, torture, and death or exile of each member of Sophia's inner circle. Golitsyn was banished to Siberia. Shaklovity was executed. Tsar Ivan, at Peter's request, asked Sophia to leave the Kremlin and take up residence at Novodevichy Convent; she was not required to become a nun, and was given a large suite with luxurious furnishings and a complement of servants. But she could be visited there by no one except her female relatives. She was, in effect, being returned to the terem, a devastating fate for the first woman ever to rule Russia.

Peter was so intimidated by Sophia that he refused to leave Troitsky and take up his seat in Moscow until she was safely behind the walls of the convent. Later in life, he described his sister as "a princess endowed with all the accomplishments of body and mind to perfection, had it not been for her boundless ambition and insatiable desire for governing." It was, of course, characteristic of the time and place where Sophia lived that ambition and the will to govern were perceived as flaws in her character. But in her regency, Sophia Alekseyevna had thrown open a door that would not be shut again for more than a hundred years. Peter himself would be succeeded by a woman, Catherine I. She would be followed, with only brief interruptions by short-lived male rulers, by Anna, daughter of Ivan; her own daughter, Elizaveta; and finally, Catherine the Great, the last of Russia's great autocrats.

Chapter Two: The Tsar in Europe

The All-Drunken Synod

For the first five years after Sophia's regency ended, from 1689 to 1694, Peter's day to day life was not remarkably different than it had been when his sister was running the government. He was less interested in governing Russia than he was in being able to do whatever he liked without Sophia or his mother Natalya or his wife Eudoxia interfering. To his brother and co-tsar Ivan, Peter delegated all the ceremonies and formalities the tsar was required to participate in. Affairs of government were left to his uncle Lev Naryshkin, who was made chief foreign minister, Tikhon Streshnev, who was in charge of domestic policy, and Boris Golitsyn, cousin of Sophia's advisor Vasily Golitsyn. Natalya Naryshkina also wielded influence over government affairs, though she lacked Sophia's energy and ability. Patriarch Joachim of the

Orthodox church was her chief personal advisor. The government of Sophia Alekseyevna and Vasily Golitsyn was seen as having been corrupted by foreign influence, and the Naryshkin party was reactionary and xenophobic by way of contrast. Ironically, the tsar in whose name they served continued to spend all of his time mingling with foreigners from the German Quarter. Peter's chief interests were what they had always been—shipbuilding, European technology, and military strategy—and there was nowhere else in Moscow he could pursue them.

The German Quarter had been established by tsar Alexei, who decreed that foreigners should not live within the boundaries of the Orthodox city of Moscow. (It was occupied by English, French, and Dutch persons, as well as by Germans; the Russian word for "German" was applied broadly to all foreigners.) The borders of Russia had long been closed to outsiders, but when the English king Charles I was beheaded by

Cromwell, Alexei was so incensed that he opened the borders of Russia to royalist refugees from England and Scotland—which was how the Scottish Catholic Mary Hamilton had arrived in Moscow to become the patroness of Natalya Naryshkina. The sophisticated Vasily Golitsyn, whose tastes inclined to the European, had also opened the foreign suburb to Huguenots fleeing France after the Edict of Nantes, which permitted Protestants to live peacefully alongside Catholics, was revoked by Louis XIV. Skilled foreigners, such as doctors and schoolmasters and engineers, were also permitted to live in the foreign suburb, since Russia was in dire need of their skills.

Russian suspicion of foreigners was directly responsible for the fact that so few Russians had this kind of skilled training. Russia was as isolated by the Orthodox religion as it was by landlocked geography. Europeans were anathema because Protestants and Catholics alike were heretics; their languages, learning, culture, and technology were similarly suspicious because they derived from heretical teachings. Peter's attachment to foreigners was highly distressing to his subjects, even to his mother, though Natalya Naryshkina was more influenced by European culture than any previous tsarina. It was to separate Peter from foreign influences that his mother had tried to limit the amount of time he spent studying ship building at Lake Pleschev with his Dutch mentors.

Now that Peter was tsar, however, no one could prevent him from keeping company with foreigners, and since he took no interest in governing his country, he had no other claims on his time. In the German Quarter, European expats lived in much the same style they had lived at home—they had their own theaters, restaurants, bookshops, and a steady influx of information from their connections in Europe. Peter had frequented this oasis of modern civilization since he first met the Dutch engineer Timmerman as a boy. Now that he was tsar, he more or less took up permanent residence there. Drinking in pubs, hearing news of the west, keeping company with women who were not confined to the terem, whetted Peter's appetite for first-hand knowledge of distant lands. The foreigners he kept company with all had opinions about Russia and how it compared their homelands. The tsar of Russia was deeply interested in this outside perspective.

This was not to say that all of Peter's companions were foreigners. He still kept company with the motley band of peasants, serfs, and boyars that had formed the nucleus of the Preobrazhensky Guards back when it was merely the unusually well-equipped nursery-yard of a child who liked to play at war. These included boys and young men close to Peter's own age, and mature men with a long history of state service who took it upon themselves to earn Peter's trust, recognizing that the young tsar would need the guidance of experienced statesmen when he chose to take up the responsibility of governing. All together, this group of about two hundred men and boys from a diverse array of backgrounds came to be known as the All-Mad, All-Jesting, All-Drunken Synod, or the Jolly Company for short. One scholar has referred to this company as "the government of Russia in brutally drunken disguise." They followed Peter wherever he went, and because all power in an autocracy derives from proximity to the autocrat, this band of hard-drinking revelers functioned as a combination of advisory cabinet and peripatetic military headquarters. Peter invented joke-ranks to bestow on members of the Company, such as "the Polish King" and "Prince-Caesar", but because the ranks indicated that the bearer stood high in the tsar's favor, they translated to real power.

Peter's pious Orthodox subjects were scandalized by the Company's openly blasphemous sense of humor. Some concluded that Peter was under evil influence; others decided that he was simply the anti-Christ. The adolescent appeal of a 24/7 partying lifestyle is probably obvious, but it is also understandable why Peter was most comfortable when he was surrounded by experienced soldiers in his pay and retainers who were intensely loyal to him personally. Even his boyhood military games make sense when one considers the effect that the Streltsy revolt must have had on him as a child. The fact that he was tsar had not shielded him when the Streltsy stormed the Kremlin and slaughtered his relatives. From childhood, he knew that he could never be supremely powerful so long as he was dependent on ignorant, suggestible soldiers whose loyalty to the tsar only made them more dangerous in the hands of sophisticated politicians who knew how to manipulate them. Peter would be a soldier himself—no honorary commander, but one who had worked his way through the ranks and come to understand the lives, struggles, and dangers his men were subjected to. And during the earliest, most vulnerable years of his reign, he would live amongst the men who knew him best and were loyal, not so much to the tsar of Russia, as to the man Peter, their companion and drinking partner.

Archangel

"For some years I had the fill of my desires on Lake Pleschev, but finally it got too narrow for me... I then decided to see the open sea, and began often to beg the permission of my mother to go to Archangel. She forbade me such a dangerous journey, but, seeing my great desire and unchangeable longing, allowed it in spite of herself."

> Peter the Great, *preface to Maritime Regulations*

Peter's time with the Jolly Company was not devoted exclusively to fast living and hard drinking. He still visited Lake Pleschev to work in his boatyard, but what had been a fine hobby for a boy felt like amateurism and playacting to the adult tsar. Peter dreamed of sailing the open sea much the way a young person today might dream of being an astronaut—the ocean was just as vast and unknowable as deep space, just as full of peril. There was only one port in all of Russia that communicated with the sea: Archangel, in the far Arctic north, choked with impenetrable ice for eight months of the year. During the summer months, it stood harbor to ships from England, Holland, the German states—none of the ships at Archangel were Russian. The city traded fur, wheat, caviar, and other goods of Russian origin for English wool,

German lace and wine, and other European luxuries.

Because the journey from Moscow to Archangel was over a thousand miles long, no tsar had ever visited the port city in person, but Peter was determined to go. His mother Natalya was equally determined he should not—Peter scarcely seemed to have a hobby that didn't make his subjects fear for his life, and the prospect of the tsar undertaking a sea voyage was unthinkable. What if he should be lost at sea? How could he be reached in case of some disaster at home? Peter promised her that he only wanted to sail the harbor, and that he would not venture beyond the mouth of the bay into the vastness of the Arctic ocean.

But then, in February of 1694, tsarina Natalya Naryshkina died, at the age of forty-two. Peter was so devastated by his grief that he could not bring himself to attend the lavish state funeral he arranged for her. "I dumbly tell my grief and my last sorrow," he wrote to friends in Archangel, "about which neither my hand nor my heart can write in detail, without remembering what the Apostle Paul says about not grieving for such things, and the voice of Edras, 'Call me again the day that is past.' I forget all this as much as possible, as being above my reasoning and mind, for thus it has pleased the Almighty God, and all things are according to the will of their Creator. Amen. Therefore, like Noah, resting awhile from my grief, and leaving aside that which can never return, I write about the living." The living, Peter's letter went on, should continue work on the ship Peter had begun building in Archangel the previous summer, the keel of which he had fashioned with his own hands. Natalya had been the only person, inside the family or out of it, with enough influence over Peter to persuade him to what he did not wish to do. Now that she was dead, he had no one left to please except himself. By April, he was in Archangel again, sailing his newly-completed ship *St. Paul* in the frigid waters. The maiden voyage of the *St. Paul* nearly ended in the capsizing of the ship and the drowning of the tsar, but he managed to steer the ship safely to port in the Unskaya Gulf.

Azov

On February 9, 1696, Peter's brother and co-tsar Ivan died at the age of twenty-nine. Peter was fond of his brother and had always treated him with the respect due to the senior of the two tsars. Nonetheless, his death made little difference to Peter, save that there was no more danger of Sophia or her allies attempting to depose him to rule in Ivan's name as regent. He was now the sole supreme ruler of Russia.

At the time of Ivan's death, Peter was busy constructing a fleet of Russian ships to launch an attack against the Ottoman empire at the fortress of Azov on the Black Sea. His sister Sophia, and her foreign minister Vasily Golitsyn, had prosecuted an unsuccessful war against the Ottomans by sending a land force over the steppes. Peter, however, fueled by ambition to make Russia a maritime power, divided his forces between land and river. The first siege of Azov, in 1695, was unsuccessful because Russian boats could not maintain control of the waterways to prevent the Turkish garrison from being resupplied. In preparation for the second siege, Peter converted the town of Voronezh on the Don River into a shipyard, where he ordered the construction of the Azov Flotilla: twenty-three galley ships, along with two ships of the line and four fire ships.

Still in his early twenties, Peter was famous not only for his enormous height and strength but for his incredible physical energy; these qualities were useful to him as he personally directed construction and building of the ships under the tutelage of master carpenters. The second siege began on May 28. By July 19, the garrison at Azov had surrendered. This was the first significant military victory by Russian forces since the reign of Peter's father, Alexis. Peter immediately set to work converting Azov into an Orthodox city, replacing mosques with churches; even more significantly, he ordered the construction of a Russian warm water port on the north shore of the Sea of Azov. But in order to have access to the wider world, Russia would have to control the strait of Kerch, between Azov and the Black Sea, which was still in Turkish hands.

In order to achieve such a victory, Peter would need a proper fleet of sea-going vessels, not just galleys and barges. In other words, Russia would need a navy. Peter outsourced the cost of this endeavor to the wealthiest of his subjects. Every great monastery, each of the greatest landowners, all would be responsible for constructing one ship apiece. And in order that the Russian navy would not have to be solely dependent on the drafted expertise of foreigners, Peter ordered fifty men from the most powerful families in Russia to travel west at their own expense in order to learn from experts how to build and navigate these ships. This decree horrified the families of the men he had selected; hardly any Russians traveled to Europe, and it was well known that the west was full of corrupting influences. But Peter had even more shocking news to relate: he was sending high-ranking Russian ministers as ambassadors on a diplomatic mission to the courts of the kings of Europe. Furthermore, he would be traveling with them—not in state, with the royal trappings that befit a monarch in a foreign country, but incognito, under the name Peter Mikhailov. Peter had been the first Russian tsar ever to make a saltwater voyage; now he would be the first tsar ever to leave Russia in peacetime.

The Great Embassy

"He turned his whole mind to the construction of a fleet... A suitable place for ship-building was found on the River Voronezh, close to the town of that name, skillful shipwrights were called from England and Holland, and in 1696 there began a new work in Russia—the construction of great warships, galleys and other vessels. And so that this might be forever secured in Russia, and that he might introduce among his people the art of this business, he sent many people of noble families to Holland and other states to learn the building and management of ships; and that the monarch might not be shamefully behind his subjects in that trade, he himself undertook a journey to Holland; and in Amsterdam at the

East India wharf, giving himself up, with other volunteers, to the learning of naval architecture, he got what was necessary for a good carpenter to know, and, by his own work and skill, constructed and launched a new ship."

> Peter the Great, *Maritime Regulations*

Speculation abounded, both in Russia and abroad, regarding Peter's decision to visit Europe unencumbered by the trappings of his rank. To his horrified Russian ministers, Peter explained that he had made a vow to visit the tomb of St. Peter in Rome, to give thanks for having been safely delivered from the storm that nearly killed him during his first sea voyage. Some thought he was probably motivated by nothing more than the desire to amuse himself; Peter Mikhailovich, no doubt, would have more fun knocking about Europe than would Tsar Peter I, Autocrat of All Russia. The simplest explanation for his decision to travel incognito is probably that Peter had never been comfortable with the pomp and ceremony that came with being tsar. He had avoided ceremonial functions whenever possible, leaving them to his brother when Ivan was alive, ignoring them entirely afterwards. In his play regiments as a boy, and in the All-Drunken Synod afterwards, it had suited Peter to elevate his companions to mock-ranks of the most exalted stations, and to address them the way his boyars addressed him, as a groveling slave pathetically grateful for their notice. By pretending to be something other than he was, Peter gained a perspective on the world that is rarely granted to royalty. And it kept people guessing. It is easy to hide one's true feelings behind customary obsequiousness; no doubt Peter found it useful to take the measure of a man when he had upset their preconceived notions of how to behave around royalty.

His incognito aside, the purpose of Peter's Great Embassy, as it was called, was primarily to solidify his alliance with other Christian kings against the Ottoman empire. He would need their support when his navy was at last finished and he went to war against the Turks for the Strait of Kerch. Peter would travel first to Poland, Russia's historic enemy, which had become their first and principle ally against the Turks. He would travel next to Austria, and then to Venice, which had supplied Russia with master shipbuilders to assist in building the Azov Flotilla. Along the way, he would visit Holland and England, to further his knowledge of shipbuilding. The great Protestant nations were also the greatest shipwrights in the western world. Having spent so much of his childhood in the German Quarter of Moscow, Peter felt far more comfortable amongst Protestants than most Orthodox Russians did. He also intended to recruit as many experienced shipbuilders and sailors as could be enticed to resettle in Russia, and to purchase instruments and materials necessary in constructing Russian ships. Peter's sojourn to western Europe was to last eighteen months; it was the last great educational experience in his self-administered curriculum as a student of European society and technology.

Historian Robert Massie describes the company that set off on the Great Embassy thus:

"Chosen to escort the ambassadors [Francis Lefort, Fedor Golovin, and Prokofy Voznitsyn] were twenty noblemen and thirty-five young Russian 'volunteers' who, like those dispatched in previous months, were going to England, Holland and Venice to learn shipbuilding, navigation and other nautical sciences... To complete the Embassy, there were chamberlains, priests, secretaries, interpreters, musicians... singers, cooks, coachmen, seventy soldiers and four dwarfs, bringing the total above 250. And somewhere in the ranks was a tall young man, brown-haired, dark-eyed, with a wart on the right side of his face, whom the others addressed simply as Peter Mikhailov. For members of the Embassy to address him as anything else, to reveal that he was the Tsar, or even to mention that the Tsar was present with the Embassy, was punishable by death."

(In fact, all of Europe knew that Peter was six feet, eight inches tall, in an era where the average man stood significantly less than six feet. He was easy to pick out. But pretenses had to be maintained.)

Riga, Courland, and Brandenburg

On his way to Europe, Peter passed through Riga, in Swedish Livonia, in the Baltic. Since Riga's defenses existed for the exact purpose of keeping Russia at bay, the presence of the Russian tsar, who took a more or less scholarly interest in sketching the city's fortifications, made the Swedes fairly nervous. At one point, a Swedish soldier threatened to fire his musket at the tsar if he did not cease drawing sketches and taking measurements. Obviously, the soldier knew only that the person he was threatening was a foreigner, not that he was the Russian tsar. Peter escaped unharmed and the soldier, who had only been doing his duty, was not punished, but Peter left Riga with a bad taste in his mouth. Three years later, he would attack the city in the opening move of the Great Northern War, using the rude treatment he had received there as an excuse.

Peter's journey took him next to the Duchy of Courland, a semi-independent possession of Poland, and then to Königsberg, in Brandenburg. The Embassy had learned its lesson in Riga; Peter technically maintained his incognito, but his identity was discreetly related to pertinent officials, so that no more diplomatic mishaps would occur. Peter negotiated a loose treaty of mutual assistance with Frederick, Elector of Brandenburg, and took lessons from a captain of artillery, learning to fire cannon with precision. The Embassy's next destination was Holland, but by this time word had spread throughout Europe that Peter was coming, and it was difficult to make rapid progress; all the ceremony he had hoped to avoid by traveling under a pseudonym was making its way to him regardless. He was waylaid by the Electresses of Hanover, Sophia and her daughter Sophia Charlotte, both of them well-educated, sophisticated, and intellectual, even by European standards. Peter had never met women of their kind before, and when they invited him to dinner, he found himself so bashful that he covered his face with his hands and murmured, "I don't know what to say." But they soon put him at his ease and enticed him into drinking and dancing. In the words of Electress Sophia:

"The Tsar is very tall, his features are fine, and his figure very noble. He has great vivacity of mind, and a ready and just repartee. But, with all the advantages with which nature has endowed him, it could be wished that his manners were a little less rustic.... He was very gay, very talkative, and we established a great friendship for each other, and he exchanged snuff-boxes with my daughter... We regretted that we could not stay much longer, so that we could see him again, for his society gave us much pleasure. He is a very extraordinary man. It is impossible to describe him, or even to give an idea of him, unless you have seen him. He has a very good heart, and remarkably noble sentiments. I must tell you also that he did not get drunk in our presence, but we had hardly left when the people of his suite began to make ample amends. He is a prince at once very good and very bad; his character is exactly that of his country. If he had received a better education, he would be an exceptional man, for he has great qualities and unlimited natural intelligence."

Holland

At the time of Peter's visit in 1697, Holland was, despite its diminutive size, the wealthiest, most technologically advanced, and socially sophisticated nation in Europe, and it was one of the chief destinations on his trip west. All commercial sea traffic originating in Europe and traveling to points west and north was routed through the port cities of Rotterdam and Amsterdam. For Peter, whose imagination was wholly preoccupied with ships and sea travel, his journey to Holland had something of the nature of a pilgrimage. In Courland and Brandenburg, Peter had been little more than a diplomatic tourist, but in Holland, in the small city of Zaandam, he proposed to make his home for many months as a student of Dutch shipbuilders. He traveled ahead of the rest of the Great Embassy, arriving in Zaandam with only a handful of chosen companions out of the retinue of two hundred. There, he encountered, by chance, a blacksmith named Gerrit Kist, who had helped teach Peter in Moscow when he was a boy. Overjoyed to meet an old friend in a foreign country, Peter took up lodgings in a tiny wooden house next to Kist's, and got himself hired as a common workman at a nearby shipyard. When he had spare time, he visited the families of other Dutchmen he had known in Moscow, rewarding them and dining with them and giving them news of their scattered relations.

Unfortunately for Peter, word of his arrival spread quickly, and once again, his remarkable physical characteristics—his immense height, the small wart on his cheek, and the involuntary twitching of his features under stress which sometimes extended to contractions of the limbs—made him all too easy for the average person to recognize. He was only able to spend about a week in Zaandam before it became impossible for him to work or observe work being done, due to the massive crowds of people thronging along the docks to get a glimpse of the Tsar of Muscovy. He was forced to quit the city entirely and retreat to Amsterdam, where the rest of the Embassy was soon due to arrive. It was in Amsterdam, rather than Zaandam, that Peter would linger for months as an apprentice ship builder.

In order to spare Peter the crowds of curious spectators, the burgomaster of Amsterdam arranged for him to live and work in the private shipyards of the East India Company, where the public could not go and which were screened from view. There, he worked daily, helping to build a frigate which was christened *The Apostles Peter and Paul*. In the evenings, he read and replied to correspondence from Moscow. Before, he had taken little interest in the operations of his own government. But just prior to his departure, a few members of the Streltsy had been arrested and executed on a treason charge. Any hint of treachery from the Streltsy ignited Peter's fury; he had never forgotten how they had terrorized him and murdered his family when he was a boy. Now that he was far from home, he took new interest in what was befalling Russia in his absence, especially where the Streltsy were concerned.

Peter sometimes took breaks from the shipyards to study with leading Dutch experts in other fields: architecture, drawing and engraving, engineering, book printing, anatomy, medicine, and surgery. He learned how to perform a number of simple surgical procedures himself, such as tooth extractions, and was so eager to ply his skills that his companions on the Embassy learned not to complain of toothache within the tsar's hearing—otherwise, they risked Peter ordering them to submit themselves to his learning and his bag of sharp surgical instruments.

In 1698, after four months of working in a shipyard, Peter found himself better at handling an axe and saw than he had been before, but he still had not learned what he had come to Europe to learn. His goal was to discover simple, consistent principles of shipbuilding that could be reduced to blueprints and mathematical formulas that could be passed on to inexperienced carpenters in Russia who had never seen a frigate or a saltwater vessel larger than a yacht. But Dutch shipbuilding, though accomplished, was not yet consistent or scientific, and Peter was left dissatisfied. He decided to travel next to London, and wrote to William of Orange for permission to make the visit while maintaining his incognito. William and Peter had met several times in Amsterdam, and William responded to his request by gifting him with the fastest yacht ever produced by a European shipyard. Delighted, Peter once again left his Embassy behind, and set sail for England.

England

Peter had learned to idolize the fierce William of Orange as a boy, hearing tales from Dutch carpenters in the German Quarter of how the Dutch prince had repelled the French invasion of Holland by destroying the dikes and flooding the lowlands to keep the French armies out of Amsterdam. Some twenty years later, William and his wife Mary had become joint monarchs of England during the Glorious Revolution, making William de facto head of a European coalition whose goal was to check the expansionist ambitions of Louis XIV.

William was considerably older than Peter, and very unlike him in temperament, but he was flattered by Peter's admiration, and he was curious about the young tsar who was so keen to acquire first-hand knowledge of European technologies and crafts. More importantly, Peter cherished a vivid animosity against William's bitter enemy, Louis XIV, and though Peter had been unsuccessful in persuading the Dutch heads of state to support his war against the Turks, having a common enemy provided firm diplomatic footing for Peter's visit to the island nation. London was next in importance to Amsterdam among European port cities, the Thames providing access to a steady stream of merchant ships from all over the world. When Peter came to visit London, he was, in accordance with his own wishes, given a modest house along the river with doors that opened directly onto the water.

While Peter was in England, rumors began to spread that the young Russian tsar was not a firm believer in the Orthodox faith, meaning that he (and through him, all of Russia) might be a prospect for conversion to Protestantism. The Bishop of Salisbury and the Archbishop of Canterbury had a long conversation with him at the request of William of Orange. The Bishop wrote the following description of Peter long after the tsar had departed England:

"I waited often on him, and was ordered both by the King and the archbishop and bishops to attend upon him. I had good interpreters, so I had much free discourse with him. He is a man of very hot temper, soon inflamed, and very brutal in his passion; he raises his natural heat by drinking much brandy, which he rectified himself with great application. He is subject to convulsive motions all over his body, and his head seems to be affected with these. He wants not capacity, and has a larger measure of knowledge than might be expected from his education, which was very indifferent; a want of judgment with an instability of temper, appear in him too often and too evidently. He is mechanically turned, and seems designed by nature to be a ship-carpenter rather than a great prince. This was his chief study and exercise while he stayed here. He wrought much with his own hands, and made all about him work at the models of ships. He told me how he designed a great fleet at Azov, and with it to attack the Turkish empire; but he did not seem capable of conducting so great a design, though his conduct in his wars since this time has discovered a greater genius than appeared at that time. He was desirous to understand our doctrine, but he did not seem disposed to mend matters in Muscovy [by converting to Anglicanism]; he was, indeed, resolved to encourage learning, and to polish his people by sending some of them to travel in other countries, and to draw strangers to come and live among them. He seemed apprehensive still of his sister's intrigues. There is a mixture of both of passion and severity in his temper. He is resolute but understands little of war, and seems not at all inquisitive that way. After I had seen him often, and had conversed much with him, I could not but adore the depth of the providence of God, that had raised up such a furious man to so absolute authority over so great a part of the world."

The bishop seems not entirely disappointed to discover that Peter was not a candidate for conversion, as though his "furious" nature made up for his spiritual heterodoxy. As other high churchmen of Europe were to discover, Peter was interested in different sects of Christianity, not because he wished to abandon Orthodoxy, but because he was interested in comparing the moral philosophies of different religions. The Quaker sect interested him more than the Church of England; he attended a few services at Quaker meeting houses, and declared that "whoever could live by such a doctrine would be happy." The implication, of course, was that he was not such a person. He was desirous of loosening the stranglehold of Orthodox xenophobia over the Russian people. It had become evident to him that a major reason for Amsterdam's prosperity was the religious tolerance practiced by the Dutch; a port city that hosted visitors from all over the world, Amsterdam became a haven for Huguenots fleeing France after the revocation of the Edict of Nantes, and foreigners of all faiths met with similar tolerance there. No matter how many warm water ports Orthodox Russia might one day control, they would never thrive as Amsterdam did unless a similar welcome was extended to persons of all cultures and faiths.

Peter had intended only a short visit to England before returning to Holland and making his way thence to Vienna. But he kept finding reasons to prolong his stay. He toured Westminster Abbey, Windsor Castle, and Hampton Court; he visited the Greenwich Observatory, Woolwich Arsenal, and the Tower of London, where Peter made an exhaustive study of the Royal Mint. Recently, the Mint had begun to produce coins with striations around the edges, to prevent them from being trimmed and the metal melted down into new coins. Peter would adopt this innovation when he began to reform Russian coinage a few years after his return from Europe. In addition to all this, William gave Peter complete access to the English fleet and allowed him to inspect it in a special review. Afterwards, Peter was invited to observe a session of Parliament, during which he concluded that, although he could never tolerate such limitations on a monarch's power, "it is good to hear subjects speaking truthfully and openly to their king. This is what we must learn from the English!"

Vienna

Peter departed from England at last on May 2, 1698, aboard the *Royal Transport*, the yacht William had given to him that promised to be the fastest ever built. After slight detours along the river to visit yet more magnificent English ships, he set sail for Amsterdam, where the majority of his Embassy was still waiting for him. They had not been idle; they had recruited almost seven hundred Dutch naval officers, engineers, technicians, doctors, and similar to resettle in Russian, to ply their trades and train young Russians in them. Two weeks later, the entire Embassy was en route to Vienna.

Vienna was the heart of both the Holy Roman Empire—a loose assembly of German and Italian states dating back to the reign of Charlemagne in the ninth century—and the Habsburg Empire. The two empires were united in the person of Leopold I, Emperor of the Holy Roman Empire, Archduke of Austria, King of Bohemia, and King of Hungary. Leopold was in his late fifties, more akin to William of Orange in his melancholy, dour temperament than the energetic Peter of Muscovy. His holy destiny, Leopold believed, was to uphold the Catholic church; minor matters, such as the governing of the states over which he nominally ruled, were best left to minor persons. Leopold's court was principally concerned in upholding protocol. All men, all kings and princes of the earth, were inferior to the Emperor, save for the Pope; tsar Peter, however vast his remote eastern kingdom, was not his equal. Leopold's courtiers had heard rumors of Peter's rough, unpolished manners from their envoys to other European states; it took them days to come to an agreement with Francis Lefort on the exact manner in which the incognito tsar would be received by the emperor, and they were in mortal dread lest the irrepressible youth run roughshod over all their protocol.

True to their predictions, Peter did not abide strictly by the instructions passed on to him by his ambassadors, but his manners had acquired a little more polish during his travels than rumors indicated, and he managed to make himself agreeable to Leopold, especially when he accepted only half the sum the Austrians offered to defray the Embassy's expenses while in Vienna. Peter spent little time alone with the emperor, though he met with other princes of the Catholic church while he was there. It was well known that Peter's next destination was Italy; first Venice, to study their famous boats and canals, then Rome, to visit the tomb of St. Peter. As had happened in England, rumors began to circulate that Peter might be persuaded to turn his back on the Orthodox church. It was even whispered that he intended to visit Rome for the express purpose of being received by the Pope as a convert. Accordingly, Peter was visited by Cardinal Kollonitz, Primate of Hungary, who found that none of these rumors were true. He wrote an interesting description of Peter, however, which enlarges our picture of him during his European sojourns:

"The Tsar is a tall young man from twenty-eight to thirty years of age, with a dark complexion, proud and grave, and with an expressive countenance. His left eye, his left arm and left leg were injured by the poison given him during the life of his brother [NB: the Cardinal is referring to the rumors, spread by Sophia, that Ivan was the victim of an assassination attempt by the Naryshkins]; but there remains of this now only a fixed look in his eye and a constant movement of his arm and leg. To hide this, he accompanies this involuntary motion with continual movements of his entire body, which by many people, in the countries which he has visited, have been attributed to natural causes, but really they are artificial. His wit is alert and quick; his manners, closer to civil than savage. The journey he has made has improved him greatly, and the difference from the beginning of his present travels and the present time is obvious, although his native coarseness still appears; chiefly in his relations with his followers, whom he holds in check with great severity. He has a knowledge of history and geography and he desires to know more about these subjects; but his strongest interest is in the sea and ships, on which he himself works manually."

Peter's principle purpose in visiting Vienna was to rally the Austrians against the Turks. Traditionally, the Habsburgs considered themselves the defenders of the east-west border separating the Muslim Ottomans from Christian lands. But Austria's proximity to the Ottomans sometimes resulted in a more complex diplomatic relationship between the two empires. Perpetual hostility and warfare simply wasn't practical. At present, Austria was on the verge of entering peace talks with the Turks, a peace which would not benefit Russia but which would leave Austria free to conserve its resources in the event of war with France, which, during the reign of Louis XIV, was never far from the horizon. The best Leopold could do for Peter was suggest that he return to Russia as soon as possible, make his war against the Turks, and win Kerch. Treaty negotiations would not begin for some time, but once they were concluded, each monarch would have to be content with the territory they already held.

Peter was dissatisfied, but it was the best he could hope for under the circumstances. In July of 1698, he began making preparations to leave for Venice. Just as he was on the point of leaving, however, he received an urgent warning from Moscow: the Streltsy were in revolt once more. There were no further details, and Peter, fearing the Streltsy as he did, instantly imagined the worst. He and his retinue instantly reversed course, leaving the road to Venice behind and making for Poland. Along the way, he received a second letter, this one indicating that the rebellion had been put down. Peter was relieved, but he decided to continue in the direction he was heading. His attitude towards government had been immature and apathetic when he left Moscow the previous year, but he heard learned a great deal since then. He had seen the world, spoken with and observed other rulers in their own courts and countries, and the inner workings of his own state had become more interesting to him in the process. It would have been horribly ironic if, just as he was making preparations to drag Russia into the eighteenth century by the long beards of its boyars, a second Streltsy revolt had destroyed his court and put Sophia back on the throne in his place. Peter decided it was time to go home; on the way, however, he would have to go through Poland.

Poland

Augustus, King of Poland, (also called Augustus the Strong) was the Elector of the German state of Saxony. Electors were roughly equal to princes, so titled because they possessed the right to vote in the election of the Holy Roman Emperor—although, since the title of Emperor always went to the next Habsburg heir, electors were more traditional than functional in their duties.

Poland itself was technically a republic. It was ruled by kings who were elected by a parliament of Polish nobles, called the Diet. Traditionally, only foreigners were elected, because this prevented any of the ruling families of the Polish nobility from establishing a dynasty. Polish elections were therefore an irresistible opportunity for foreign powers to meddle in Polish politics. In the late 17th century, Poland rivaled Russia in size, but its population was disunited; it included a slim majority of Catholic Poles, but also large numbers of Orthodox Lithuanians and Russians, Protestant Germans, and a substantial number of Jews. This disunity prevented Poland from building a grand army or playing a significant role in European politics. Nonetheless, as Russia's nearest neighbor, Poland was worth Russian attention. Augustus, who had been king for less than a year, was the candidate Peter had favored in the most recent election, and now Peter was going to be a guest at his court.

Unlike Leopold or William, Augustus was a man after Peter's own heart: tall, strong, good humored, and fun loving, with a penchant for hard drink and ribald jokes. And they had something even more important in common: the newly-elected king had his sites fixed on war with Sweden, whose king had just died, leaving the fifteen-year-old Charles XII on the throne. Since Sweden held sway over much of the Baltic, this aligned with Peter's own ambitions to secure access to warm water sea ports. By the time Peter left Poland, bringing to an end the eighteen-month sojourn of the Great Assembly, he had secured the Polish alliance that would make the greatest military enterprise of his reign possible.

Chapter Three: The Great Northern War

Return to Moscow

Historian Robert Massie summarizes the accomplishments of the Great Assembly in Europe thus:

"Peter and his ambassadors had succeeded in recruiting more than 800 technically skilled Europeans for Russian service, the bulk of them Dutchmen, but also Englishmen, Scots, Venetians, Germans, and Greeks. Many of these men remained in Russia for years, made significant contributions to the modernization of the nation and left their names permanently inscribed in the history of Peter's reign.

"More important was the profound and enduring impression that Western Europe made on Peter himself. He had traveled to the West in order to learn how to build ships, and this he had accomplished. But his curiosity had carried him into a wide range of new fields. He had probed into everything that caught his eye—had studied microscopes, barometers, wind dials, coins, cadaver and dental pliers, as well as ship construction and artillery. What he saw in the thriving cities and harbors of the West, what he learned from the scientists, inventors, merchants, tradesmen, engineers, printers, soldiers and sailors, confirmed his early belief, formed in the German Suburb, that his Russians were technologically backward—decades, perhaps centuries, behind the West.

"Asking himself how this had happened and what could be done about it, Peter came to understand that the roots of Western technological achievement lay in the freeing of men's minds. He grasped that it had been the Renaissance and the Reformation, neither of which had ever come to Russia, which had broken the bonds of the medieval church and created an environment where independent philosophical and scientific inquiry as well as wide-ranging commercial enterprise could flourish. He knew that these bonds of religious orthodoxy still existed in Russia, reinforced by peasant folkways and traditions which had endured for centuries. Grimly, Peter resolved to break these bonds on his return."

Peter and his followers returned to Moscow on September 5, 1698. He was in high spirits, eager to begin implementing the reforms he had devised on his travels. The first of these reforms came as a sudden and terrible shock to his ministers and nobles: as they came to greet the tsar on his arrival, Peter embraced them heartily, then produced a knife and began to cut off their beards. To Russian men of the late seventeenth century, this was more than an aesthetic alteration. Until recently, it had been a crime. Ivan the Terrible had outlawed the cutting of beards, and the law had only changed during the reign of tsar Alexei, Peter's father. Furthermore, the Patriarch of the Orthodox church had declared the cutting of beards to be a mortal sin. To Peter, this was foolishness. He intended to break the bonds of ancient, stultifying tradition across all levels of Russian society, and naturally those closest to him must set the first example. He had never worn a beard, and in Europe he had observed that long flowing beards were a stereotype attributed to Russians, an amusing symbol of their backwardness and isolation from European culture. Peter would not be laughed at anymore. Those who insisted on keeping their beards were permitted to pay a tax, which gained them a token with the image of a beard engraved upon it, above the words "tax paid", but even this would not save a boyar from Peter's displeasure if he came into the tsar's presence without being clean-shaven. At first, the rule regarding beards applied only to nobles, but eventually peasants were required to shave as well. Since the Orthodox church did not alter its position on shaving being a sin despite Peter's new rule, many peasants kept their beards after cutting them off, tied up in string, so that they could be buried with them and present them to the apostles in the afterlife, to prove they had once been faithful.

No sooner had Peter done away with Russian beards than he turned his interdiction onto Russian clothing. Traditional Russian apparel for men included loose embroidered shirts and pants tucked into boots with pointed, curling toes, underneath embroidered caftans with extremely long sleeves and fur-lined robes with sleeves that dragged the ground for outdoor wear. For women, clothing was much the same, including embroidered blouses and sarafans, similar to a modern pinafore dress or jumper, embroidered caftans, and long flowing veils to cover the hair and the face when outdoors. Such voluminous clothing served an eminently practical purpose during the severe Russian winter, which was far colder than anywhere in Europe, but indoors they were clumsy and ungainly. Sometimes the robes were so long that one could not walk in them without tripping; sleeves were liable to catch on goblets of wine or fall into food dishes.

Peter attacked the Russian caftan as he had attacked the Russian beard: with a knife. Nobles who came into his presence in traditional dress were likely to have their sleeves cut off by the tsar. By 1700, men were required to wear the waistcoat and breeches of their European counterparts; women were to wear bonnets, dresses, and petticoats. (Interestingly, the corset, the indispensable foundation garment of European women until the early twentieth century, was unknown in Russia at this time. When Peter danced with the Electress of

Hanover, he felt the corset under her dress when he grasped her waist, which led him to remark innocently that German women had devilishly hard bones, to the great merriment of the other guests. Peter's new laws for female dress in Russia did not extend to requiring corsets, possibly because there were very few corset-makers in Russia at the time.) Peter's subjects were not as resistant to changing their clothing as they had been to cutting their beards—women in particular found European garments pleasant and freeing in comparison to what they had been used to—but the first few winters after Peter's return to Moscow must have been difficult for them, as men struggled to keep warm with their calves shielded only by stockings.

There was one last change Peter was determined to carry out immediately after his return to Moscow. His marriage to Eudoxia Lopukhina had resulted in the birth of his heir, the tsarevitch Alexei, who was now eight years old.

But it had also resulted in a complete alienation of Peter's affection for his simple, traditional wife, who neither liked nor understood his foreign habits or foreign friends. Peter had mingled with German and Dutch women as a boy in the German Quarter, but they were mostly prostitutes, barmaids, or the wives of carpenters and workmen. During his travels, however, he had made the acquaintance of many Western women of his own rank, women who were well-educated, politically sophisticated, and accustomed to social freedoms that made them the intellectual equals of men.

Eudoxia, through no real fault of her own, had always bored Peter. He had married her only at his mother's insistence, and his mother had chosen Eudoxia for the very qualities that made her loathsome to Peter—her piousness, her traditional Russian femininity. Unfortunately for the luckless girl, Natalya had come to dislike Eudoxia as well when she failed to secure Peter's affections and divert him from foreign influences. Eudoxia had her son, but she had no other support at court, since Peter's sister Natalya and Ivan's widow Praskovia were enthusiastic supporters of his Western reforms.

Now that Peter had a broader experience of female company, he was determined to end his marriage in the only way that an Orthodox husband could—by persuading Eudoxia to become a nun. It is evident that he had made up his mind on this subject long before his return to Russia. In Vienna, Peter had requested that no toasts be made to the tsarina's health, and he had written to his advisors that they should begin to speak to Eudoxia of retiring to a convent, a delicate task they were reluctant to undertake. Peter was not pleased to find Eudoxia still in the palace upon his return. When he attempted to persuade her to become a nun, she resisted, saying that she could not abandon her responsibilities towards Alexei. In the end, Peter simply removed Alexei from Eudoxia's household, sending him to live with Natalya, and had Eudoxia sent to a convent over her own protests. After a couple of years, she gave up hope of a reconciliation, and took holy orders as the nun Helen.

The Downfall of the Streltsy

During Sophia's reign, the Streltsy had been the elite of the Russian army. They had a certain style of living to which they were accustomed: quartered in Moscow during peacetime to safeguard the Kremlin and the tsar, they had so little to do in their official capacity that they mostly lived at home with their wives and families, running small businesses on the side. After Sophia was deposed to a convent, however, Peter revoked most of their traditional privileges. This was what had led to the revolt that brought

Peter hastily back to Moscow. Peter had sent the Streltsy to hold Azov after it was conquered, bestowing upon his own Preobrazhensky and Semyonovsky Guards, who had proven far more effective fighters, the honors and rewards the Streltsy felt they had earned.

The Streltsy continued to regard themselves as the guardians of all that was holy, Orthodox, and authentically Russia. This was the attitude which had emboldened them to lay siege to the Kremlin sixteen years before, and it led them to regard Peter with suspicion. He didn't act like a real tsar. A real tsar was more a living icon than a human being, a remote figure who kept to his palace and appeared to the public only on solemn occasions, dressed in his glittering robes like an emissary from heaven. Ivan, Peter's brother, had been such a tsar. Now Ivan was dead, Peter was in Europe doing who knows what, and they were being ordered to garrison remote outposts far away from their rightful place in the heart of Moscow, near their families.

On June 9, a Streltsy regiment of two thousand men began to march toward the city, striking terror in the hearts of all those who remembered or had heard of the bloody chaos of the last revolt. While ordinary people prepared to flee Moscow, the Preobrazhensky and Semyonovsky Guards, under the command of General Patrick Gordon, rode out to face them. The Streltsy were outnumbered; Gordon recommended that they desist before their actions carried them beyond the possibility of mercy or pardon. Fighting broke out, but it was over in under an hour, as the loyal troops lay waste to the Streltsy with cannon fire. Those who survived were bound in chains and interrogated under torture until they confessed that they had intended to sack Moscow, burn the German Quarter, depose the absent Peter, and make Sophia Alekseyevna regent again, this time for the tsarevitch Alexis.

The plot had been unsophisticated, and unconnected to machinations on the part of any high-ranking official, but Peter, whose fury against the Streltsy was unbridled, feared that some deeper scheme was afoot, probably instigated by Sophia, whom he still feared as the only person in Russia capable of challenging him. When he returned to Moscow, the arrested Streltsy were subjected to hideous torture. Johann-Georg Korb, secretary to the newly established Austrian embassy in Moscow, wrote an account of this second Streltsy revolt. It is partly derived from secondhand accounts, but it portrays vividly the intensity of Peter's feelings:

"How sharp was the pain, how great the indignation, to which the tsar's Majesty was mightily moved, when he knew of the rebellion of the Streltsi, betraying openly a mind panting for vengeance! He was still tarrying at Vienna, quite full of the desire of setting out for Italy;

but, fervid as was his curiosity of rambling abroad, it was, nevertheless, speedily extinguished on the announcement of the troubles that had broken out in the bowels of his realm. Going immediately to Lefort (almost the only person that he condescended to treat with intimate familiarity), he thus indignantly broken out: 'Tell me, Francis, son of James, how I can reach Moscow by the shortest way, in a brief space, so that I may wreak vengeance on this great perfidy of my people, with punishments worthy of their abominable crime. Not one of them shall escape with impunity. Around my royal city, which, with their impious efforts, they planned to destroy, I will have gibbets and gallows set upon the walls and ramparts, and each and every one of them will I put to a direful death.' Nor did he long delay the plan for his justly excited wrath; he took the quick post, as his ambassador suggested, and in four weeks' time he had got over about three hundred miles without accident, and arrived the 4th of

September, 1698—a monarch for the well disposed, but an avenger for the wicked.

"His first anxiety after his arrival was about the rebellion—in what it consisted, what the insurgents meant, who dared to instigate such a crime. And as nobody could answer accurately upon all points, and some pleaded their own ignorance, others the obstinacy of the Streltsi, he began to have suspicions of everybody's loyalty... No day, holy or profane, were the inquisitors idle; every day was deemed fit and lawful for torturing. There were as many scourges as there were accused, and every inquisitor was a butcher. ...The whole month of October was spent in lacerating the backs of culprits with the knout and with flames; no day were those that were left alive exempt from scourging or scorching; or else they were broken upon the wheel, or driven to the gibbet, or slain with the axe...

"To prove to all people how holy and inviolable are those walls of the city which the Streltsi rashly meditated scaling in a sudden assault, beams were run out from all the embrasures in the walls near the gates, in each of which two rebels were hanged. This day beheld about two hundred and fifty die that death. There are few cities fortified with as many palisades as Moscow has given gibbets to her guardian Streltsi. (In front of the nunnery where Sophia was confined) there were thirty gibbets erected in a quadrangle shape, from which there hung two hundred and thirty Streltsi; the three principal ringleaders, who tendered a petition to Sophia touching the administration of the realm, were hanged close to the windows of that princess, presenting, as it were, the petitions that were placed in their hands, so near that Sophia might with ease touch them."

When Korb published his memoirs of his life in Russia, from which the above is excerpted, Peter was furious. He had attempted to keep any foreigners in Moscow from learning what happened deep in the bowels of his fourteen torture chambers. To Peter, it was necessary to inflict such hideous tortures in order to safeguard his realm and secure his throne, but he was aware that, even though western monarchs also resorted to torture to punish those convicted of treason, the sheer scale of the suffering inflicted on the Streltsy would make him seem monstrous in European eyes. He could not prevent rumors of what was happening from getting abroad—after all, any person walking down the street could hear the screams and cries of the victims. But Korb's account was damning, and Peter demanded that the Habsburg emperor suppress its publication in Vienna.

In the end, all 1,714 of the Streltsy who had been arrested were tortured daily (except for Sundays) for a month and a half. There was no relief from the pain; men who confessed to one offense were re-interrogated the next day regarding different charges. Those who came close to death were nursed back to health so that they could be tortured for longer. Peter also ordered the interrogation and torture of the chambermaids who attended Sophia at the Novodevichy Convent, hoping to find evidence that the Streltsy had been acting on her orders. Under these tortures, one person indicated that Sophia had written secret letters to the Streltsy, urging their revolt. Peter went to see Sophia in person to question her about her involvement. She told him that she played no part in recent events, and it seems that Peter believed her. Nonetheless, he forced her to take vows and become a nun, in order to keep her movements more restricted in the future. She died at Novodevichy six years later.

When the interrogations were finished, there were so many prisoners to execute that they had to be killed in batches throughout the fall and winter. Twelve hundred men were executed, their families exiled. A few hundred were spared due to their youth, but had their faces branded or their noses cut off to mark them as traitors permanently. By 1708, all of the Streltsy, including the sixteen regiments that had no involvement in the revolt, had been permanently disbanded, scattered, exiled, and forbidden from ever bearing arms again. Once they had prided themselves on being the guardians of the tsar himself; now that place was supplied by the Preobrazhensky Guards, the regiment Peter had formed with his childhood friends and playmates.

Francis Lefort died of a sudden, unidentified illness in March of 1699, at the age of forty-three. He had been Peter's constant companion since Peter was a boy; it was Lefort who had infused Peter's play regiments with real military discipline. It had been Lefort's idea for Peter to travel to Europe, and he himself had been the chief ambassador of the Great Embassy. More importantly, out of all his retainers, Lefort was the man Peter trusted most. He had been near Peter at every important stage of his life since the regency of Sophia. Peter ordered a state funeral and commanded all his boyars to attend. Then, in November of the same year, Peter suffered the death of Patrick Gordon, the Scottish general who had, like Lefort, been Peter's loyal companion since he was a child. Gordon had served three tsars, and though he had not always lived in Russia willingly, he had become the most capable officer in its army. When Gordon died, Peter was present, and he himself shut the dead man's eyes after the Catholic priest attending him performed last rites. The deaths of these two men combined with the end of Peter's European sojourn and the turn of the eighteenth century to draw a line of demarcation between the tsar's youth and his maturity.

The Great Northern War

The fleet of ships which Peter had ordered to be built (and helped to build himself) at Voronezh were never used for their intended purpose, which was to wrest Kerch away from the Ottoman empire. Instead, as peace was being negotiated between the Turks and the Western powers in Vienna, Peter dispatched Emilian Ukraintsev, his chief foreign minister, to approach Constantinople with a request to establish a permanent Russian embassy there, and to enter negotiations for Russian interests along the Black Sea. To suggest what the consequences might be if they refused, Ukraintsev made his journey to Constantinople in a brand new forty-six-gun frigate named *The Fortress*, escorted by twelve other Russian ships. This was Russia's first display of might at sea. The Turks were astonished. Ukraintsev was accepted as a diplomatic envoy, and negotiations began after three months. Peter requested that

Russian merchant ships be allowed to sail through the strait from Azov to the Black Sea. This, the Turks were adamant they could not do, but they agreed to the permanent embassy, the cancellation of Russian tribute payments to the Khan of Crimea, which Peter had been paying to keep the Tatars from raiding Ukraine, and to allow Orthodox clergy access to the tomb of the Holy Sepulcher in the Holy Land, which was then under Ottoman control.

This was not what Peter had hoped for as little as two years ago, but it was of less significance to him now, as he approached the dawn of the eighteenth century with new hopes. His conversations with Augustus, king of Poland, had enkindled new ideas for how Russia might gain access to the Baltic.

Charles XII

In the late seventeenth century, Sweden was an empire, comprising the Baltic states of Finland, Karelia, Estonia, Ingria, and Livonia, and German ports such as Pomerania, Stettin, Stralsund, and Wismar. Sweden's authority over the Baltic sea was absolute, and its German territories gave it potential access to anywhere in western Europe. It was ruled by Charles XII, who had inherited the throne at the age of fifteen after the sudden death of his father from stomach cancer. Charles XII is now a legendary figure in Swedish history, and is considered second only to Peter himself in the list of century's greatest rulers. The following description of Charles from his childhood is taken from a biography written by the French philosopher Voltaire after Charles' death:

"[Charles XI] married, in 1680, Ulrica Eleanora, daughter of Ferdinand, King of Denmark, a virtuous princess worthy of more confidence than her husband gave her; the offspring of this marriage was Charles XII, perhaps the most extraordinary man ever born, a hero who summed up in his personality all the great qualities of his ancestors, and whose only fault and only misfortune was that he carried them all to excess. It is of him, and all that is related of his actions and person, that we now purpose writing. As soon as he had some knowledge of Latin they made him translate Quintus Curtius; he took a liking to the book rather for the subject than the style. The tutor who explained this author to him asked him what he thought of [Alexander the Great]. "I think," said the Prince, "that I would like to be like him." "But," was the answer, "he only lived thirty-two years." "Ah!" replied the Prince, "and is not that long enough when one has subdued kingdoms?" These answers were reported to the King his father, who exclaimed, "That child will excel me and he will even excel Gustavus the Great.'

"[After Charles became king at age fifteen] three strong princes, taking advantage of his extreme youth, made simultaneous plans for his ruin. The first was Ferdinand IV, King of Denmark, his cousin; the second Augustus, Elector of Saxony and King of Poland; the third, and most dangerous, was Peter the Great, Tsar of Russia."

It would be unfair to accuse Peter of any personal animosity against the young Charles, but he happened to rule an empire which had long disputed with Russia over possession of Ingria, Estonia, and Livonia, all of which bordered Russia, and Karelia, which also bordered Finland. The Swedish had been the enemies of the Muscovites since the thirteenth century, when Moscow was only a sovereign city-state. Russia's landlocked status was due to the fact that the entire northern coast of the continent above Moscow was under Swedish dominion. Peter's father, tsar Alexis, had attempted to drive the Swedish back west into the Scandinavian peninsula, but he had been forced to give up the enterprise when a second war broke out between Russia and Poland. Peter, like Alexis, regarded the Baltic states as rightfully Russian, and now, having been forced to give up on his Black Sea enterprise, he was ready to take possession of them again.

The Coalition

Even so, the enterprise that was to become known as the Great Northern War was not entirely Peter's own idea. Frederick IV of Denmark was eager to recapture Scania, the southernmost province of the Swedish peninsula, which had once been a Danish possession. And Augustus of Poland, the third member of the coalition, had an even more complex scheme in hand. Having been elected king of Poland, he wished to convert the republic into an absolute monarchy, with himself as the founder of a new hereditary dynasty. Augustus had been approached by a Livonian noble by the name of Johann von Patkul with an offer that might make this wish a reality. Patkul had been condemned for treason by the Swedish king for speaking out against the seizure of Livonian estates by the Swedish crown. He had come to the decision that if the Polish were to take Livonia, they would allow Livonian nobles a greater degree of freedom than they had enjoyed under their Swedish masters. Patkul's argument was that, if Augustus, who was Elector of Saxony in addition to being king of Poland, used his Saxon soldiers to conquer Livonia, he could then present Livonia to the Polish Diet as a sort of gift, in exchange for being made hereditary king.

Between them, so the plan went, Augustus and Frederick of Denmark would engage the Swedish forces on three fronts. Denmark would attack Scania and drive Swedish troops out of the German principality of Holstein-Gottorp to the south; Augustus would attack Livonia. Peter, tsar of Russia, was invited into the enterprise almost as an afterthought, and not without some hesitation. There was always the chance that Peter would seize Livonia for himself, if they were not careful.

Peter agreed that he would join Denmark and Poland in the offense against Sweden, but the date was left unspecified, and there was a catch: the Russian ambassador in Constantinople was in the process of negotiating a thirty-year temporary peace treaty between Russia and the Ottoman empire, and until it was formalized, he could spare no troops to fight the Swedish, lest negotiation prove unsuccessful and war break out with the Turks. Confident of their success, Frederick and Augustus did not wait for Russian assistance before Saxony attacked Livonia (without going through the formality of declaring war first, an insult that Augustus's cousin, Charles XII, would not forget) and Denmark attacked Holstein-Gottorp. On August 8, 1700, Peter received word from his ambassador that the peace had been secured in Constantinople. He had spent the past six months preparing Russia for war, and now at last he knew who he was going to war with.

When the formal declaration of war against Sweden was read out in Moscow, the *casus bellum* was phrased in simple terms that simple Russians could understand. The tsar was going to reclaim Ingria and Karelia, which had belonged to Russia before the Romanov dynasty was founded. And he was going to attack Livonia, because it was there, in the city of Riga, that Peter had been treated with such churlish inhospitality at the beginning of his Great Embassy to Europe three years before.

War

All three members of the coalition, Peter, Augustus, and Frederick, had been in agreement on at least one point: now was the opportune moment to break the might of the Swedish empire, because Charles XII was still only eighteen, and it was assumed that he would be flustered and over-awed by the sudden assault.

But as the coming conflict was to prove, Charles XII was "the most daring and aggressive soldier of the age." One historian writes that he was "anxious for battle, at any time and at any odds." In other words, no one was prepared, or could have foreseen, that the teenage king whose youth and inexperience was supposed to open the doors of his empire to foreign aggressors would prove to be nothing less than a military genius. When Charles received news that the Polish king had attacked Livonia, he addressed the Swedish Parliament, declaring that, because Augustus had broken his word to honor existing treaties between Poland and Sweden, Sweden occupied the moral high ground. This was an important distinction to the deeply religious Charles, and to his subjects, because it meant that God was on their side and would uphold the justice of their cause.

Charles attacked the Danes first, leaving the defense of Livonia to the garrison in Riga. He was supported by Holland and England, as William of Orange wanted the conflict in the north ended quickly, so that Europe would not grow distracted while Louis XIV threatened to annex Spain. The Danish had attacked the Swedes in Holstein-Gottorp, but the Swedish, Dutch, and English coalition struck directly at Copenhagen, on the island of Zealand. Frederick IV was entirely unprepared for an assault against his capital; Copenhagen surrendered under siege, and Denmark was forced to sign a peace treaty with Sweden and withdraw its soldiers from Holstein. The entire campaign lasted only two weeks. Now Charles, who made a firm policy of only fighting wars in one place at one time, was free to turn his attention north.

The Polish siege of Riga had not been immediately successful, and by the time Charles had won his swift, decisive victory in Denmark, Augustus was ready to retreat for the winter. Peter, meanwhile, was two weeks into the siege of Narva, a coastal city close to the Estonian border with Ingria. Charles was spoiling for a fight, and since Augustus had forsaken the field of battle, his sights landed on Narva. This was more than mere belligerence; if the Russians took Narva, then Estonia, Ingria, and Livonia would fall to them in short order. Even if Charles had not been determined to fight *someone*, the Swedish regiment at Narva was badly in need of relief.

When Peter received word that the Swedish army was approaching, he was prepared for a long wait before any fighting broke out. The Swedish forces were outnumbered by the Russians four to one, and they had just finished an exhausting march over hundreds of miles of territory. They would need time, he thought, to build encampments and regain their strength. Anticipating weeks of inaction, Peter left for the Russian city of Novgorod to confer with Augustus of Poland, whose retreat from Riga had come as an irritation and a disappointment.

He was due for an astonishing surprise and unwelcome surprise, however. The very next day, in the middle of a snowstorm, Charles ordered his beleaguered forces to charge the Russian siege line. Panic broke out amongst the untested, undisciplined Russian soldiers, who, in the words of one observer, "fell like grass." Surrender followed, but there were so many more defeated Russian soldiers than there were victorious Swedes that the Swedish officers were nervous that the Russians would notice their numerical advantage and mount a counterattack. Instead, the Russians departed east for Russia, leaving most of their officers behind as prisoners of war.

Years later, after Peter's great victory against the Swedish at Poltava, he wrote of the aftermath of his defeat at Narva:

"Our army was vanquished by the Swedes—that is incontestable. But one should remember what sort of army it was. The Lefort regiment was the only old one. The two regiments of Guards…had never seen any field fighting, especially with regular troops. The other regiments consisted—even to some of the colonels—of raw recruits, both officers and soldiers. Besides that, there was the great famine... In brief, it was like child's play [for the Swedes]. One cannot, then, be surprised that against such an old, disciplined, and experienced army, these untried pupils got the worst of it. The victory then was indeed a sad and severe blow to us. It seemed to rob us of all hope for the future, and to come from the wrath of God. But now, when we think of it rightly, we ascribe it rather to the goodness of God than his anger; for if we had conquered then, when we knew as little of war as of government, this piece of luck might have had unfortunate consequences... That we lived through this disaster, or rather this good fortune, forced us to be industrious, laborious, and experienced."

In the wake of his victory, Charles had a choice: either to follow the retreating soldiers and invade Russia itself, or to invade Poland and redress his grievance against Augustus. At this juncture, it becomes evident why Peter later considered his defeat at Narva to be a blessing.

Russia was now the laughingstock of Europe. There could be little glory for Charles in winning additional victories against the Russians; he stood to gain nothing except Peter's humiliation, which he had already achieved. The Saxon army of the Polish king, on the other hand, was technically undefeated, which made it a more tempting challenge for a soldier like Charles. Furthermore, the political climate in Poland was auspicious for an invasion. Augustus's relationship with his Polish subjects was growing uneasy. He had not won the promised victory over Livonia; instead, he had angered the Swedes and risked their retaliation. The Primate of Poland, Cardinal Radiejowski, had written to Charles, declaring that Augustus had made war against Sweden without the consent of the Polish people, who wanted only peace with his country. Charles replied by asking the Poles to convene the Diet, dethrone Augustus, and choose another king.

When this request met with no definitive response, Charles decided to invade Poland, with the intent of forcing a new election. This was the best possible outcome for Peter. Had Charles not been diverted by Poland, he would have found the road to Moscow virtually unobstructed—Peter's armies were in no condition to repel an invasion. Though he was deliberately choosing to invade the stronger of his two enemies, Charles believed he was on the path to another rapid victory. Instead, he became embroiled in a war that would last for six years—six years of reprieve for Russia that Peter would put to excellent use.

St. Petersburg

In 1702, while Charles was distracted by Poland, Russian forces seized the Swedish fortress of Nöteberg; this gave them undisputed possession of the Neva river, and, through it, a permanent foothold on the Baltic Sea. Conquest of Ingria followed in 1703. Anticipating that the Swedish would soon try to wrest these possessions from his grasp, Peter set about making his claim on them in as permanent a fashion as can be imagined—by building a fortress at the mouth of the Neva, and, around the fortress, a city, which he named St. Petersburg. More convenient than Archangel, blessed with slightly warmer winters, Peter's city was the Russian answer to Amsterdam, to London, to Venice. Some part of him had loathed Moscow and the Kremlin since the Streltsy revolt in his childhood. A new capital, named for his patron saint, with its face turned to the sea, was Peter's attempt to remake Russia in his image.

Construction of St. Petersburg began on May 16, 1703. The work was done by men with shovels and pickaxes. Wheelbarrows were unknown in Russia, so the workers had to clear the worksite of dirt with their hands. According to legend,

Peter marked the exact spot where they were to begin working with a cross, where he buried a box containing the bones of St. Andrew, Russia's patron saint. As he did this, an eagle, the emblem of the house of Romanov, came to rest in a tree over Peter's head, presumably to bless the enterprise. The Swedish army returned to the region that summer, and every summer thereafter, to try to drive the Russians out, but they were too firmly encamped. The new shipyards at Lake Ladoga, south of Karelia, was providing Peter with ships—not enough of them to break the Swedish blockade on the river, but enough to enable them to hold their ground until the winter ice forced the Swedish to retreat.

Once there was enough city to live in, Peter used his autocratic privilege to populate it, mostly by forcing people to relocate from their homes in Moscow. Furthermore, the wealthiest families were required to build beautiful, elaborate homes "in the English style" along the left bank of the Neva. The number of serfs the family owned determined how large the house had to be. All of this had to be undertaken at their own expense. It was similar to the tactic Peter had used to get the Azov fleet built, and it was a tactic that probably only would have worked in Russia, where the nobility were accustomed to bowing to the tsar's whims, however eccentric.

St. Petersburg was reckoned a miserable place to live for the first decade or so of its existence, despite the fact that Peter considered it his "Eden." It was prone both to flooding and fires; crops were not grown there, so nobles and peasants alike had to pay ruinous mark up on most kinds of food. And there was little to do by way of entertainment. The tsar might derive endless amusement from proximity to the water, but not one of his subjects would set foot on a boat unless it was under direct orders. Even the Swedish found it impossible to understand why Peter clung so tenaciously to such a marshy, inhospitable plot of land. They assumed that the city would eventually fail. Only a few people—Peter himself, his close friend Alexander Menshikov—understood that one day St. Petersburg would rank among the greatest, most beautiful cities in the world.

Martha Scavronskaya

"After this advantage, the Russian general marched onwards, laid the whole country under contributions, and took the little town of Marienburg, on the confines of Ingria and Livonia. There are several towns of this name in the north of Europe; but this, though it no longer exists, is more celebrated in history than all the others, by the adventure of the empress Catherine.

"Among the prisoners [taken from Marienburg] was a young woman, a native of Livonia, who had been brought up in the house of a Lutheran minister of that place, named Gluck, and who afterwards became the sovereign of those who had taken her captive, and who governed Russia by the name of the empress Catherine.

"There had been many instances before this, of private women being raised to the throne; nothing was more common in Russia, and in all Asiatic kingdoms, than for crowned heads to marry their own subjects; but that a poor stranger, who had been taken prisoner in the storming of a town, should become the absolute sovereign of that very empire, whither she was led captive, is an instance which fortune never produced before nor since in the annals of the world."

Voltaire, *The History of Peter the Great*

As Voltaire indicates in this excerpt, it was customary in Russia for the tsar to marry beneath himself socially, always to a daughter of one of the less powerful boyar families. This practice ended with Peter himself. Peter's victory in the Great Northern War established Russia as a force to be reckoned with on the European stage, and a direct consequence of this was that the marriage-market of European nobility was opened to the Romanovs for the first time. Peter's son, Alexei, would be married to a foreign princess, as would all of Peter's successors. For a time, Peter even dreamed of marrying his daughter Elizaveta to the French king, a scheme which proved unsuccessful but which could not even have been dreamed of by his predecessors.

As the newly styled emperor of Russia, the unwed Peter might potentially have made a bargain for the hand of a foreign princess of his very own. But as it happened, his choice for

Russia's first empress was made much closer to home. He looked no further than his own bedchamber.

One of Peter's oldest friends was Alexander Menshikov, a piroshky vendor who was introduced to him by Francis Lefort when Peter was a young man wandering the suburbs of Moscow in search of adventure. Menshikov had risen high in Peter's service, proving his loyalty by working alongside him as a shipbuilder in Amsterdam. After Lefort's death, Menshikov had become Peter's most trusted advisor. He played important roles in the battle of Azov and had helped to conquer the Swedish fortress of Nöteberg; Peter rewarded him for this service by appointing Menshikov its governor. They were best friends for many years; Peter addressed him as "Alexashka".

After his victory against the Swedish, Peter paid a visit to Menshikov's household in Moscow, where he met a nineteen-year-old peasant girl named Martha Scavronskaya. Not much is known of her background, save that she was of Livonian-Lithuanian stock and had been taken into the home of a Lutheran minister named Gluck as a child after her parents died of the plague. She was not brought up as a daughter of the Gluck family; rather, she earned her keep by working for the family as a laundrywoman and scullery maid.

By the time Martha was seventeen, her guardians were eager to marry her off, lest their son, whom they intended for greater things, fall in love with her. Martha was accordingly married to a Swedish dragoon whose name has been recorded as Johann Abbe or Johan Cruse. Whether this marriage was agreeable to Martha or not is unknown; in either case, she was with her husband for only eight days, as they became separated when Marienburg surrendered to the Russians. Martha was left to make her own living. She began doing laundry for Russian soldiers, and at some point thereafter she entered Menshikov's service. Menshikov was notorious for keeping a large number of female servants, mostly serfs, who performed both domestic and sexual duties for him and for any guests he might be entertaining. Menshikov was not a pleasant individual, but Martha apparently found something to like in him, because they were close for the rest of their lives. According to some versions of the story, she was Menshikov's mistress when she caught Peter's eye. Whether he was her lover or merely her master, Menshikov immediately ceded his claims on Martha in favor of the tsar.

Martha's rapport with Peter was instant. Though she was illiterate, he prized her for more than her beauty. She was clever, cheerful, fun-loving, patient with his foibles, tolerant of his roving eye, and capable of keeping up with Peter and his friends in their drunken revels. Crucially, she was an able nurse when Peter had one of his "fits", the stress-induced spasms of his face and limbs that sometimes made him painfully self-conscious in the company of strangers. Peter made her his mistress immediately after their first meeting in 1703, though she continued to live in Menshikov's house for several years. Together, Peter, Catherine (as she became known after her conversion to the Orthodox faith), Menshikov, and Menshikov's mistress Darya, were often seen around Moscow. Within nine months, Catherine, gave birth to the first of the twelve children her union with Peter would ultimately produce.

A German diplomat who met Catherine in 1717 described her thus:

"The Tsaritsa was in the prime of life and showed no signs of having possessed beauty. She was tall and strong, exceedingly dark, and would have seemed darker but for the rouge and whitening with which she covered her face. There was nothing unpleasant about her manners, and anyone who remembered the Princess's origins would have been disposed to think them good... She had a great desire to do well... It might be fairly said that if this Princess had not all the charms of her sex, she had all its gentleness... During her visit to Berlin, she showed the Queen the greatest deference, and let it be understood that her own extraordinary fortune did not make her forget the difference between that Princess and herself."

Voltaire writes that "nothing was more common in Russia...than for crowned heads to marry their own subjects", but in fact, it was not at all usual for a tsar to marry a woman whose origins were as obscure as Catherine's. The tsar married boyars, not peasants. More importantly, Catherine was not even Russian. Her elevation was as shocking and distressing to Peter's more traditional subjects as the cutting of their beards. But their objections fell on deaf ears. Peter could not do without her. The only serious hesitation he had in marrying her lay in the fact that Eudoxia still lived. Though she was a nun now, the insult to her family might be more than his subjects would tolerate. Nonetheless, they were married in a private ceremony in the new city of St. Petersburg in 1708. The marriage remained secret until four years later, in 1712, when Peter and Catherine were married again in a lavish public ceremony. Altogether, they had twelve children, six girls and six boys, though only two of their offspring, both daughters, survived to adulthood.

Chapter Four: Poltava and Alexei

"In the early years of war—indeed, throughout his reign—Peter was constantly on the move... During this time, the Tsar was never more than three months in a single place. Now in Moscow, now in St. Petersburg, now in Voronezh; then on to Poland, Lithuania, and Livonia, Peter traveled incessantly, everywhere inspecting, organizing, encouraging, criticizing, commanding... Traveling back and forth over the immense distances of his empire, the Tsar broke every precedent before the eyes of his astonished people. The time-honored image of a distant sovereign, crowned, enthroned and immobile in the white-walled Kremlin, bore no resemblance to this black-eyed beardless giant dressed in a green German coat, black three-cornered hat and high, mud-spattered boots, stepping down from his carriage into the muddy streets of a Russian town, demanding beer for his thirst, a bed for the night and fresh horses for the morning."

Robert Massie, *Peter the Great*

Abdication of Augustus of Poland

In 1705, after years of indecisive conflict between the Swedish army of Charles XII and the Saxon army in Poland, the Polish Diet bowed to pressure and elected a new king, Charles's handpicked protégé, Stanislaus I. But the election was considered illegitimate by many Poles—not only had it been transparently manipulated by Charles, but Stanislaus was crowned in Warsaw, rather than the traditional coronation seat of Krakow, with a new crown and scepter ordered and paid for by Charles. Furthermore, Augustus refused to abdicate, which meant that Charles was obliged to leave some ten thousand Swedish troops in Poland when he turned his sights back on Peter—who, in 1704, had reversed his disastrous defeat at Narva and seized the fortress. Swedish troops advanced on Grodno, a fortress town in Lithuania, some four hundred miles away from Moscow. But Peter, wishing to preserve his army, abandoned Grodno rather than engaging the Swedish in open battle. When Charles attempted to follow their retreat, the bridge over the river Neman collapsed. By the time the Swedish had navigated around it, the Russians had made a clean escape.

In 1706, Charles forced Augustus's hand by invading Saxony, where he met with little resistance, as the Saxons were tired of Augustus's long war on foreign soil and were not willing to see the electorate pillaged by Swedish soldiers for the sake of their erratic Elector. Without the support of the Saxon army, Augustus was no longer a useful ally to Peter. He traveled to meet Charles in person, promising to abdicate from the Polish throne in exchange for mercy towards Saxony. To Peter, this meant one thing. Charles was well-known for fighting only one war at a time. His attempted attack against

Grodno had been unsuccessful in part because his heart was not in it, not while matters with Augustus in Poland remained unsettled. When Peter received word of Augustus's abdication, however, he knew that Charles's next move would be an attempted invasion of Russia—of Moscow itself.

The Great Northern War had begun with a coalition of Russia, Poland, and Denmark arrayed in opposition against the Swedish empire. Now, only Russia remained. Peter was without allies. Charles was inclined towards single-minded vendettas; any nation that attacked him must be prepared to fight to the bitter finish, because Charles would end the war on no other terms. Now, with the Swedish army positioned in Saxony, near the heart of western Europe, no European monarch would dare risk angering him by coming to Russia's assistance, even if they wished to. The Protestant powers, England, Holland, and the German states, were particularly concerned that Charles might make an alliance with France, which would radically unbalance the distribution of power in Europe. It was in their best interests for Charles to engage distant Russia, and leave the French to them. And though Peter made tentative overtures of peace towards Charles, they had little common ground from which to negotiate. Peter would not surrender St. Petersburg upon any persuasion, and St. Petersburg's position at the mouth of the Neva effectively cut Sweden's Baltic possessions in half, disrupting communications and lines of supply. Charles could make no concession on this point.

Besides all of this, Charles was eager to face the Russian army in open battle once more. He had heard rumors of the extraordinary reformation of the Russian army that had taken place since the first battle of Narva, and he looked forward to the opportunity to face them in open battle. There was a certain strain of fanaticism in his character; not only would a negotiated peace fail to satisfy him, but so would a victory that consisted only in restoring the Baltic states to the Swedish empire. These were the two options that lay before him—either a Baltic offensive, or an arduous campaign to the heart of Russia, crossing thousands of miles overland. He opted for the latter, over the concerns of his generals, for reasons that were more mystical and personal than pragmatic. Peter must be utterly and decisively ruined; God had chosen Charles for that mission. Moscow itself must be seized, and a puppet tsar of Charles's choosing installed in the Kremlin.

Invasion

Though Charles attempted to confuse Peter regarding his chosen route by ordering military actions in the Baltic, Peter was not taken by surprise. He had been anticipating and preparing for a Swedish invasion of Moscow for years; indeed, he had feared that it would follow swiftly after his defeat at Narva. Since 1707, Peter had left standing orders with the Don Cossacks of the steppes to utterly destroy the countryside frontier bordering Poland as soon as Swedish troops were spotted. Advancing armies could not carry enough food and supplies with them to sustain a march of so many miles; they depended on being able to raid farms and ransack villages as they passed. Peter's goal was to leave them with no source of sustenance. In case this was not sufficient, he likewise ordered new fortifications for the city of Moscow itself.

Advancing through Poland, the Swedish made their first strike in Grodno, the fortress that commanded the Neman river. Russian troops were on their way to secure Grodno, but the Swedish beat them to it; it was so deserted that once they had taken the bridge, they allowed the few Russian soldiers present to retreat to the town unmolested. Unbeknownst to Charles, Peter himself was in residence at the fortress, conferring with Menshikov, his most capable native Russian commander. It was a near-miss with disastrous potential consequences. If Peter's person fell into Swedish hands, the war would effectively be over. Charles remained in Lithuania near Minsk throughout the winter, which was reckoned the be "the worst winter within memory"; many of his soldiers, inadequately sheltered and supplied, died of disease and cold. Though the Swedish army was famous for its hardiness in extreme winter weather, it would not be able to move again until the grasses began to thaw in June of 1708.

Poltava

"Soldiers: the hour has struck when the fate of the whole motherland lies in your hands. Either Russia will perish or she will be reborn in a nobler shape. The soldiers must not think of themselves as armed and drawn up to fight for Peter, but for tsardom, entrusted to Peter by his birth and by the people... Of Peter it should be known that he does not value his own life, but only that Russia should live in piety, glory, and prosperity."

> Peter the Great, to the Russian army before the Battle of Poltava

When decisive victory came in the Great Northern War, it came not to Charles, but to Peter, in Poltava, a small commercial town in Ukraine, some two hundred miles from Kiev. The Swedish invasion had been advancing steadily since Grodno, aided by an unexpected alliance with the Cossack Hetman, Mazeppa. Hoping that an allegiance with Sweden would lead to independence for the Cossacks in

Ukraine, Mazeppa had suddenly deserted Peter's cause and forced him to divide his focus between two enemies. But Charles too had met with setbacks. He had attempted to form an alliance with the Turks, encouraging them to seize the opportunity of reclaiming Azov, which Peter would be forced to defend. But this alliance was refused; Constantinople had already agreed to a thirty-year peace with Russia. By the spring of 1709, the Swedish army numbered less than twenty-thousand. Charles ordered Polish and Swedish reinforcements from Poland and moved into position at Poltava to await them.

Poltava's original defenses were crude earthworks, but these had been reinforced since the beginning of the war with 91 cannon and a regiment of four thousand Russian soldiers. Beginning on May 1, 1709, the Swedish army began a six-week bombardment which, on Charles' personal orders, was so meager—limited to a mere five cannon shots a day—that the

Swedish officers were baffled as to its purpose. A sustained bombardment might bring the city to its feet in a matter of hours; Charles was letting it drag on for weeks. Bit by bit the Swedish trenches were drawing closer to Poltava, but Swedish soldiers were dying every day as they crept towards the Russian defenses. Charles explained to his officers that he wished to wait for reinforcements before the walls of the city fell and open battle commenced, but this explanation did not satisfy them completely.

Across the river, the Russian army was rallying to Menshikov, who observed the Swedes weakening. Their wounds were more susceptible to infection in the warmer weather, their food was running out, and they were low on powder and ammunition, to the point that they were scavenging in the grass for musket balls fired at them by the Russians, which they might reuse. They were also making progress, however. The commander of the garrison at Poltava, Colonel

Kelin, sent word to Menshikov that he did not expect the city's defenses to last four more weeks. Menshikov watched nervously, awaiting the arrival of the tsar, who reached Poltava at the beginning of June. For the first time, Peter did not defer to a more experienced general, but took personal charge of the battle.

Unlike Charles, whose signature in war was to defy the odds and risk everything on a single charge, Peter was cautious of his army. Charles had, in part, inherited his military strength; Peter had, in a very real sense, built his army up from the ground, starting when he was ten years old. But the Russian army outnumbered the Swedes two to one. And if Poltava fell, there would be little standing in the way of their long march to Moscow. Peter was therefore prepared to take risks.

On the night of June 14 and 15, the first forward divisions of the Russian army began to cross the river. Charles knew the advance was coming and intended to repel it, but before he had the chance, he was wounded by fire from a Russian musket. The ball struck his foot at the back of the heel and exited near the big toe. Charles, knowing that his soldiers sustained themselves on the belief that he was God's invincible servant, pretended that nothing had happened for another three hours before he allowed his doctors to treat him. The wound quickly became infected, and Charles became delirious with fever.

When Peter heard what had happened, he instantly took advantage of the confusion in the Swedish lines. The entirety of the Russian army crossed to the river's far shore. Meanwhile, as Charles lay on his sickbed, hovering between life and death, he learned that the long-awaited reinforcements from Poland were not coming.

His advisors immediately recommended that he either retreat, or entertain a peace agreement with the Russians, but Charles was unwilling to do either. He pushed for battle. Peter was not eager for a fight, but he had prepared for one. All along the road leading to Poltava from the Swedish encampment, he had ordered the construction of six redoubts (essentially, mounds of earth that provide cover for soldiers firing from the depression below), spaced about three hundred feet apart, measuring a hundred square feet apiece. When the Swedish advanced, the earthworks would force them out of formation.

When the day of the battle arrived, June 27, 1709, Charles was well enough to join his men, though he had to be carried in a stretcher guarded by twenty-four soldiers. He was so weakened that he was forced to delegate command, a necessary move that nonetheless proved the undoing of the Swedish forces. His seconds, Rehnskjold and Lewenhaupt, disliked one another; both were fearful that the other would try to take the credit for his accomplishments, so neither fully articulated his objectives to the other. The redoubts worked just as Peter had hoped; though the Swedish infantry easily swarmed over the first two, the third and fourth redoubts held six infantry battalions at bay. Before the Swedish forces even reached the city, it had lost a third of its men.

Almost as soon as the Swedish were in reach of Russian cannon, it became evident that they would not survive long without reinforcements, but no reinforcements were coming. Six battalions were still desperately attempting to conquer the third redoubt, and their commander did not realize that they were needed elsewhere, because Rehnskjold had not told him. Messengers were detached to the reserve battalion at the Swedish encampment, but they were shot down before they reached their destination. Just as Rehnskjold was preparing to retreat and regroup, the Russian army emerged from the city and its fortifications and began lining up for open battle. Never before had Peter risked his army in this fashion. The Swedish, fearing that the Russians would slaughter them from the back if they continued to retreat, wheeled about to face them. Under Charles's leadership, the Swedish had been victorious in the face of steep odds before, but Charles's leadership was the indispensable factor. The Swedish line broke quickly. Discipline broke down, the soldiers panicked, and a disorderly retreat ensued. Charles, lying prone on his stretcher, actually attempted to rally his panicking soldiers to the sound of his voice, but he could not be heard over the cannon fire.

Lewenhaupt surrendered on behalf of the Swedish three days later, on July 1, 1709. Charles, king of Sweden, had fled to Moldavia, a possession of the Ottoman empire; he would remain in exile with the Turks for the next five years. The Russians took 17,000 Swedish prisoners. The power of the supposedly invincible Swedish army was permanently broken. It was an outcome which no one in Europe had expected. From the beginning of the war, Charles's victory had been a foregone conclusion. It was with no little astonishment that the powers of the west came to understand that Russia was now the dominant power in the north. Always before, Russians had been laughed at; now, Russia would have to be watched carefully, its decisions and reactions taken into account. Peter was now an emperor. His word carried weight.

Alexei

After Poltava, Russia's status in the world changed abruptly. Among other things, the noble families of Europe were now considering the prospect of marrying their daughters to the House of Romanov in a new light. In the past, the tsars of Russia had been no more interested in marrying heretical foreign princesses than the princesses were interested in traveling to their savage country and being married to them. But Peter was now the head of an empire, and empires made alliances through marriage.

Peter's son, the tsarevitch Alexei, was nineteen years old—unusually old to still be unmarried, at least by the standards of his forebears. Peter had been trying to negotiate a marriage between Alexei and Charlotte von Brunswick-Lüneberg-Wolfenbüttel since 1707, but his overtures, though they were not rebuffed outright, had met with a lukewarm reception. Naturally, this changed after Poltava. Not only was the Duke of Wolfenbüttel suddenly eager to marry his daughter to the heir to the Russian throne; the emperor of Austria was also making inquiries regarding a marriage between Alexei and his youngest sister, Magdalena. After Poltava, Peter sent Alexei to Dresden for a year, to give a final bit of European polish to his education. There, he and Charlotte met face to face, and the final arrangements for the marriage were made.

Peter had another young relation of marriageable age to dispose of at this time: his niece Anna Ivanovna, daughter of his deceased brother and co-tsar. It was useful to be able to attract foreign princesses to Russia, but being able to make alliances by marrying Russian princesses to foreigners was more useful still. When Peter arranged a match for Anna to Frederick Wilhelm of Courland, it was the first time in Russian history that a tsarevna had been married at all, let alone to a foreigner. Unfortunately, Anna was not to prove happy in her marriage. Her husband died during the journey back to his homeland, reportedly from over-indulging during the wedding celebration. Anna begged Peter's permission to return to

Russia, but Peter would not allow it; he needed her in Courland to guarantee its neutrality in case of any future conflict in the Baltic. Anna remained there in misery and near poverty for the next twenty years. But when she did at last return to St. Petersburg, it was as Russia's second sovereign empress, Anna I.

Peter could trust Anna, however unhappy she was, to do as she was told. But he had less trust in his own son and heir. Throughout Alexei's life, Peter had alternately neglected him and made great demands of him. Alexei had been the favorite of his neglected, isolated mother Eudoxia, and when Peter returned from Europe only to banish Eudoxia to a convent and place Alexei in the care of his aunt, the boy's world had been turned upside down. Alexei did not share Peter's obsessive fascination with armies and wars; he was fond of reading and study, and probably would have made a fine priest if he had not been tsarevitch. Peter had put so much pressure on him in an effort to mold him in his own warlike image that Alexei had, at one point, tried to shoot off his own right hand with a pistol, though he only succeeded in giving himself a mild powder burn. He had suffered from depression and contemplated suicide over the years, and he coped with intolerable anxiety by drinking heavily.

Alexei's wife Charlotte died in 1715 after giving birth to a son, the future emperor Peter II. Alexei had neglected Charlotte throughout their marriage, refusing to speak to her or acknowledge her when she was in the room with him. Peter found this infuriating, both because he was fond of Charlotte, and because this behavior threatened the future of foreign marriage alliances between Russia and Europe.

The day of Charlotte's funeral, Peter wrote a letter to Alexei, outlining his disappointment in his son's character, his expectations for the future, and an ultimatum to be carried out if Alexei did not mend his ways. It has been partially reproduced below:

"You cannot be ignorant of what is known to all the world, to what degree our people groaned under the oppression of the Swedes before the beginning of the present war.

"...We submitted to this with a resignation to the will of God, making no doubt that it was He who put us to that trial till He might lead us into the right way and we might render ourselves worthy to experience that the same enemy who at first made others tremble, now in his turn trembles before us, perhaps in a much greater degree. These are the fruits which, next to the assistance of God, we owe to our own toil and to the labor of our faithful and affectionate children, our Russian subjects.

"But at the time when I am viewing the prosperity which God has heaped on our native country, if I cast an eye upon the posterity which is to succeed me, my heart is much more penetrated with grief on account of what is to happen, seeing that you, my son, reject all means of making yourself capable of governing well after me. I say your incapacity is voluntary because you cannot excuse yourself with want of natural parts and strength of body, as if God had not given you a sufficient share of either; and though your constitution is none of the strongest, yet it cannot be said that it is altogether weak.

"But you even will not so much as hear warlike exercises mentioned; though it is by them that we broke through that obscurity in which we were involved, and that we made ourselves known to nations whose esteem we share at present.

"...You mistake if you think it is enough for a prince to have good generals to act under his orders. Everyone looks upon the head; they study his inclinations and conform themselves to them. All the world knows this.

"You have no inclination to learn war, you do not apply yourself to it and consequently you will never learn it. And how then can you command others, and judge of the reward which those deserve who do their duty, or punish others who fail of it? You will do nothing, nor judge of anything, but by the eyes and help of others, like a young bird that holds up its bill to be fed.

"...I am a man and consequently I must die. To whom shall I leave after me to finish what I have partly recovered? To a man who like the slothful servant hides his talent in the earth—that is to say, who neglects making the best of what God has entrusted to him?

"...After having considered all those great inconveniences and reflected upon them, and seeing I cannot bring you to good by any inducement, I have thought fit to give you in writing this act of my last will with this resolution, however: to wait still a little longer before I put it in execution to see if you will mend. If not, I will have you know that I will deprive you of the succession, as one may cut off a useless member.

"Do not fancy that, because I have no other child but you, I only write this to terrify you. I will certainly put it in execution if it please God; for whereas I do not spare my own life for my country and the welfare of my people, why should I spare you who do not render yourself worthy of either? I would rather choose to transmit them to a worthy stranger than to my own unworthy son."

If Alexei was afraid of being cut out of the succession, he was much more afraid of exciting Peter's wrath by failing at the impossible task of transforming himself into the hearty, bluff, warlike heir his father required. Terrified and desperate, he turned to his father's advisors for advice; they, in turn, told him that it would be best if he gave his immediate assent to being disinherited. "You should renounce the succession. You are not fit for it," said one of them.

Three days after Peter's letter reached him, Alexei replied:

"I have nothing to reply [to your letter] but that if Your Majesty will deprive me of the succession to the crown of Russia by reason of my incapacity, your will be done. I even most urgently beg it of you because I do not think myself fit for government. My memory is very much weakened and yet it is necessary in affairs. The strength of my mind and of my body is much decayed by sicknesses which I have undergone and which have rendered me incapable of governing so many nations.

"...Therefore I do not aspire after you (whom God preserve many years) to the succession...even if I had no brothers as I have one at present whom I pray God preserve.

"...I put my children into your hands, and as for myself, I desire nothing of you but a bare maintenance during my life, leaving the whole to your consideration and your will."

This letter, with its tone of defeated humility, did not please Peter in the least. Like most overbearing parents who resort to threats, he had wanted to scare Alexei into doing his duty, not lose him altogether. Besides, it did not seem possible to Peter that the heir to so great a throne could really be serious in casting off all claims to the power he was born for. And even if Alexei thought himself serious, someone might persuade him to change his mind in the future. During his reign, Peter had deprived the Orthodox church of much of its former power, and he knew that his scholarly son was regarded by the leaders of the church as a potential savior. What if some "greats beards", as Peter called the Orthodox leadership, persuaded Alexei that it was his duty to strive for the succession, even after he had renounced it? Alexei might destroy everything Peter had worked for since he became tsar.

In January of 1716, Peter wrote Alexei a second letter. He upbraided his son again for failing to make himself fit for the throne, and issued a second ultimatum: either Alexei must change his ways and prepare to become a tsar in Peter's image, or he must renounce the world and become a monk. Failure to comply would result in his being branded as a traitor and a criminal.

Alexei again sought the advice of his confessor, who advised him to do as Peter commanded and become a monk. After all, he said, "they do not nail a cowl to a man's head"—meaning that

Alexei could always renounce holy orders after Peter's death. Bearing this resolution in mind, Alexei informed Peter of his decision in a face to face meeting. Either out of compassion for his son or a lingering hope that he would change his mind, Peter told him not to take any drastic steps yet. He was on the verge of making a second trip to Europe, and he was too busy making preparations to think seriously about the implications or logistics of cutting Alexei out of the succession. Peter gave Alexei six months to think over his options; at the end of that period, Peter would write again, asking his final answer.

In August of 1716, Peter wrote Alexei for the third time. Either Alexei should join a monastery, or immediately leave Russia and join Peter in Copenhagen to begin his training for the throne. Alexei was to send his answer by the same courier who had delivered this final demand. With no time left in which to deliberate, Alexei chose a third option: flight. Informing his father's ministers that he was leaving for Copenhagen, he instead went to Vienna. The emperor of Austria, Charles VI, was married to the sister of Alexis's dead wife, Charlotte, and Alexei hoped that he would shield him from Peter for the sake of the family connection. The last person Alexei saw before he left was his advisor, Alexander Kikin, who warned him: "If your father sends somebody to persuade you to return, do not do it. He will have you publicly beheaded."

Alexei had by now changed his mind about renouncing the succession. "I am weak, but I have sense enough to rule," he told the Austrian vice-chancellor. Charles VI, uncertain whether it was wisest to serve the interests of the tsar or his heir, agreed to protect him for the present, and sent him to live secretly under the guard of a garrison in a remote castle. All his needs were provided for, but he was not allowed to leave and no one was allowed to see him; all his mail was opened and read. The Austrians began to gather their own intelligence regarding the situation in Russia. They received reports that in the absence of both Peter and Alexei, "everything here is ripe for rebellion." This was not precisely true; there was a widespread feeling of resentment against Peter's reforms, but it had not reached a revolutionary pitch. Nonetheless, this report was given to Alexei, who kept it.

It was winter and Peter had reached Amsterdam before he realized that Alexei was missing. At first, it was unclear whether he had met with an accident on his way to Copenhagen; the last report anyone had of his whereabouts put his location in Danzig. But Peter soon figured out that Alexei had made an escape, a bitter humiliation for Peter as both a sovereign and a father. Eventually, his investigations traced Alexei to the castle where Charles had hidden him. The emperor was presented with a letter from the emperor requesting that Alexei be sent directly to him, with an armed guard. Charles broke the news to Alexei, who promptly became hysterical; Peter would kill him, he insisted, if the emperor did not protect him. Sympathetic to his plight, Charles sent Alexei to Naples, which was then part of the Habsburg empire, to continue in hiding and exile. The secrecy was in vain, however. Peter's agents had found tracked him to his hiding place, and when Alexei went to Italy, they followed.

Peter dispatched his minister Peter Tolstoy to see the emperor in Vienna, armed with a demand, a request, and a promise: if Charles did not surrender Peter's wayward heir, there would be consequences. But if Alexei would return, all would be forgiven. "If you are afraid of me, I assure you and I promise to God and His judgment that I will not punish you," read the letter Peter had entrusted to Tolstoy, promising reconciliation. "If you submit to my will by obeying me and if you return, I will love you better than ever. But if you refuse, then I as a father, by virtue of the power I have received from God, give you my everlasting curse; and as your sovereign, I declare you traitor and I assure you I will find the means to use you as such, in which I hope God will assist me and take my just cause into his hands."

Alexei was terrified when Tolstoy appeared to give him the letter, but once he read it, he grew calmer. He needed time to reflect. But Tolstoy, who was exceptionally sly and subtle, had realized that the key to persuading Alexei to do anything lay in first persuading his mistress, Afrosina, a serf who had accompanied Alexei to Europe in disguise as a pageboy. Tolstoy, with the cooperation of the Austrians, arrested Afrosina, then won her trust by giving her presents and promises that she would be looked after if she could convince Alexei to return to Russia. The alternative was that Tolstoy would take Alexei back by force, and what would happen to Afrosina then?

Once Tolstoy had seized Afrosina, Alexei was too shaken to do anything but agree to his father's demands. He had two conditions for his return: "that I may be allowed to live quietly in a country house and that Afrosina will not be taken away from me." Peter agreed to this. He even indicated that Alexei might marry Afrosina—so long as the ceremony took place on Russian soil.

Alexei reached Russia, under the close supervision of Tolstoy and his armed enforcers, in February of 1718. On February 3, an official ceremony took place at the Kremlin to disinherit Alexei and instate Peter's two-year-old son by Catherine, Peter Petrovich, as the new heir. The forms of the ceremony involved Alexei reading out a written confession, and Peter granting a formal, but conditional, pardon: Alexei would only be permitted to retire to his quiet country house once a thorough investigation into his flight from Russia and his actions abroad had taken place.

This was the loophole which would hang the unfortunate Alexei. It seemed to be outside the limits of Peter's imagination that his son, the heir to the throne of Russia, could have gone to such lengths merely because he was overwhelmed by the demands being made of him. Who would reject such power, when all he had to do was behave in a way that was pleasing to his father in order to retain all the privileges of a royal heir? There must be some conspiracy afoot; someone must have planted the idea in his mind, someone with larger ambitions to depose Peter and make Alexei the figurehead of a movement to reverse all the progress of Peter's reign. Alexei was asked to reveal the names of all who had assisted him in his flight. There were only two—Alexander Kikin, and his valet. Peter found this impossible to believe. In an apparent effort to make himself fully understood to his father, Alexei named seven more people, not as partners in a conspiracy, but as confidantes to whom he had related his worries about his relationship with Peter. All of these people were arrested, followed by more "conspirators", including high churchmen and Alexei's mother, Eudoxia.

Eudoxia, it was discovered, had abandoned her life as a nun a few years into her incarceration in the convent, and taken a lover. She explained that this was only because being a nun had not suited her, but Peter suspected her of having some reason to hope that she would one day be restored to her former life in the palace—if, for instance, he were deposed and Alexei made tsar. All of the accused were interrogated, and most were tortured, including nuns at Eudoxia's convent. The man who had been her lover was broken on the wheel and died after spitting in the tsar's face. Kikin and others were condemned to die lingering painful deaths, and others were condemned to simple execution or exile. As he had done when the Streltsy were interrogated, Peter attended the interrogations and participated in the torture. Such was his paranoia that many who were arrested were charged with nothing more than a vague and general feeling of sympathy for Alexei or his mother. It was an ugly, brutal affair, but the worst was yet to come.

A foreign observer in Russia wrote of the problem that Alexei still posed for Peter:

"Now comes the question: What shall be done further with the Tsarevitch? It is said that he is going to be sent to a very distant monastery. This does not seem probable to me, for the further the Tsar removes him, the greater opportunity does he give to the restless mob for liberating him. I think that he will be brought here again and kept in the neighborhood of St. Petersburg. I will not decide here whether the Tsar is right or wrong to exclude him from the succession and give him his paternal curse. This is sure: the clergy, the nobility, and the common people respect the Tsarevitch like a god."

During the interrogations and trials, and for a short time afterwards, Alexei lived near his stepmother and was seen with Peter in public. The rift between them seemed to be mended. Alexei was resigned to live in obscurity. The only requests he made were regarding Afrosina; he had not seen her since he left Naples, and he wished to be married to her as soon as possible. Afrosina, however, had been arrested as soon as she set foot in Russia, and when her belongings were searched, suggestive and incriminating documents were found. One of them was the letter Alexei had received in Austria indicating that Russia was ripe for rebellion. The others included two letters Alexei himself had written but never sent, one addressing the archbishops of the Orthodox church, the other addressing the Russian Senate:

"I believe you will be no less surprised than all the world at my going out of the country and at my residing in a place unknown at present. The continued ill-usage and the disorders have obliged me to quit my dear native country. They designed to shut me up in a convent in the beginning of the year 1716, though I had committed nothing that deserved it. None of you can be ignorant of it. But God, full of mercy, saved me by presenting to me last autumn an opportunity of absenting myself from my dear country and you, whom I could not have resolved to leave had I not been in the case where I found myself.

"At present I am well and in good health, under the protection of a certain High Person, till the time when God who preserved me shall call me to return to my dear native country.

"I desire you not to forsake me then, and as for the present, to give no credit to the news that may be spread of my death, or otherwise out of the desire they have to blot me out of the memory of mankind, for God keeps me in His guard and my benefactors will not forsake me. They have promised me not to forsake me, even not for the future, in case of need. I am alive and I shall always be full of good wishes for Your Excellencies and for the whole country."

To Peter, these were not the words of a man who had decided to give up his rights to the succession. They were not even the words of a son who had made up his own mind to live quietly abroad until his father died before returning to Russia to take up his inheritance. Rather, they seemed to open the door to conspiracy, to hint broadly that if Peter was deposed, Alexei would be happy to take his place.

But Alexei had not actually mailed the letter, so there was room for doubt.

Peter decided to interrogate Afrosina, who, either because she was too unsophisticated to realize what she was doing, or because she was too (understandably) frightened of Peter to hold anything back from him, proceeded to reveal Alexei's every secret. Robert Massie describes the damning tale which Afrosina told to Peter: "When he became tsar, he would abandon St. Petersburg and all of Peter's foreign conquests and make Moscow his capital. He would dismiss Peter's courtiers and appoint his own. He would ignore the navy and allow the ships to rot. He would reduce the army to a few regiments. There would be no more wars… The ancient rights of the church would be restored and respected."

Armed with Afrosina's information, Peter confronted Alexei again. This was to be the interview which sealed the tsarevitch's fate. Alexei claimed that the Austrians had forced him to write letters to the Senate and the Archbishops. Peter asked whether, if there had been a revolt in Moscow, as the rumors claimed, Alexei would have returned to Russia and let them make him tsar. Somewhat confusedly, Alexei said that he would have done so if Peter had been killed; because of Peter's epilepsy, he expected that Peter would die soon in any case, and if there was a coup, Peter probably would not have survived it, so it would have been Alexei's duty to return and become tsar.

This rambling answer did nothing to alleviate Peter's fears. He wrote to Charles IV in Austria and asked him why Alexei had been required to write to the Senate and the archbishops; the reply came that Alexei had not been forced, that he had written the letters himself and asked that they be forwarded to Russia through back channels, but that the Austrian vice-chancellor had thought it more prudent not to mail them. Peter questioned Alexei again, and again Alexei admitted that it was true. This was all the evidence Peter needed. The pardon Peter had granted him upon his return to Russia was invalidated by the information that had come to light since. Alexei was arrested, imprisoned in the Peter and Paul Fortress, and tried for treason. All of the accusations Afrosina had made to Peter, Peter related to the courts. Alexei himself "confessed to his father and his lord, in the presence of the whole assembly of the states ecclesiastical and secular, that he was guilty of everything described."

Alexei's ordeal was not over yet. Peter could not be certain of the right course of action when his own feelings were so deeply involved. He cast Alexei's fate upon the courts, ecclesiastical and civil, assuring them that, no matter what their verdict, they need not fear Peter's displeasure or retribution. Nonetheless, no one was in any hurry to condemn the son of the tsar to the usual fate of traitors. The church court explained that, according to Scripture, Peter would be within his rights either to have Alexei executed, since he was in violation of Old Testament law, or to show him mercy, as Christ had urged in the parable of the Prodigal Son. Dissatisfied with this answer, Peter turned to the civil court and explained that they were to treat Alexei as though he were any other Russian subject accused of treason. This meant interrogation under torture.

Over two interrogation sessions, Alexei received forty blows of the knout, during which he confessed to having wished for Peter's death. Confessions extracted under torture are notoriously unreliable, but this was probably nothing less than the truth. Peter had overshadowed Alexei's whole life; his father had placed him under such intolerable pressure that he had risked everything in an attempt to live free of his influence. Alexei, no doubt, would have been better off by far if Peter had died years ago.

Alexei's final confession brought an end to the torture; it also resulted in a sentence of execution for treason and patricide. The verdict was powerless unless Peter signed it, however, and he did not do so immediately. It is possible that he was considering a pardon. Alexei was still his son, and in his own way, Peter loved him; it was to preserve Russia that he had subjected Alexei to trials and torture. There might still be a way to save Alexei's life, even if he spent the rest of his days in prison.

Before Peter was forced to make this painful decision, however, matters were taken out of his hands. A few days after the sentence of death was passed, Alexei died in prison. In a letter which Peter wrote to the court of Louis XV, he describes how:

"In the midst of uncertain and distressing agitation, it pleased Almighty God, whose Holy Judgments are always just, to deliver by His divine grace our person and all our empire from all fear and danger and to end the days of our son Alexei, who died yesterday. As soon as he had convinced himself of the great crimes he had committed against us and all our empire, and had received the sentence of death, he was struck with a kind of apoplexy. When he recovered from this attack, having still his spirit and free word, he begged us to come to see him, which we did, accompanied by our ministers and senators, in spite of all the wrong he had done us. We found him with his eyes bathed in tears and marking a sincere repentance. He told us that he knew that the hand of God was on him and that he was at the point of accounting for all the actions of his life, and that he did not believe he would be able to be reconciled with God if he was not reconciled with his Sovereign Lord and father.

After that he entered into new details of all that had passed, feeling himself guilty, confessed, received the Holy Sacraments, demanded our benediction and begged us to pardon all his crimes. We pardoned him as our paternal duty and the Christian religion obliged us to do.

"This unexpected, sudden death has caused us a great sadness. However, we have found solace in believing that Divine Providence has wished to deliver us from all anxiety and to calm our empire. Thus we have found ourselves obliged to render thanks to God and to comport ourselves with all Christian humility in this sad circumstance."

Rumors circulated that the true cause of Alexei's death was a final session of torture, crueler than even the first two, at which Peter was present. Others said that he had been beheaded in secret, and his head sewn back onto his body for the funeral. It is more probable that he died from the delayed effects of the knout; forty lashes in a single session could kill a strong man, and Alexei was thin and sickly. But it is certainly the case that Alexei's death was convenient for Peter. He didn't have to steel himself for the task of ordering and witnessing his own son's execution. Alternatively, he didn't have to figure out how to keep Alexei alive and safe from intrigue if he chose to pardon him.

Peter's behavior throughout the whole affair with Alexei makes it easy to understand why 17th century Europeans considered Russia to be a land of barbarians and savages. And yet, torture in treason cases was normal practice in every European nation in that era. And Peter was neither the first monarch in history to grow paranoid about the succession, nor the first father in history to place unreasonable demands on his son. He wasn't even the first person to combine the two in a perfect storm of family tragedy and national crisis. Peter's actions before and during the investigation clearly indicate that he was motivated by the desire to act as he thought best for the country he had, as he believed, been entrusted by God to safeguard. It is easy to paint a picture of him as a power-mad despot who could not brook any opposition. But none of the descriptions or documents that survive from this era indicate that Peter was out of his senses with rage or unhinged by paranoia. He was methodical in investigating Alexei's actions, and he enlisted the cooperation of all his closest advisors and all the highest authorities in the nation to determine Alexei's fate. Even when the death sentence was leveled against him, Peter did not rush to sign it.

It seems evident that Peter's failure to understand Alexei's nature created a rift into which mistrust crept—and where Peter was concerned, more so than with any other Russian tsar, trust was key. The people who were closest to him and rose highest in his favor achieved their status because Peter felt that they understood him. Betrayal and bloodshed had marked him irrevocably as a child. It is common amongst people who have suffered a childhood trauma of such severity to have little tolerance for uncertainty, and Alexei represented fatal uncertainty to his father. The prospect of his succession created doubt as to whether the Russia Peter was building, which would inevitably still be a work in progress when he died, would survive after his lifetime. The ultimatum which drove Alexei to flee the country was a miscalculation on Peter's part, but it was of a sort that many fathers might have been guilty of. Had he not been an emperor, such a miscalculation would not have had such tragic consequences.

With his younger children, Peter enjoyed much closer relationships. His son Peter, known as Petrushka, was the only one of his sons who survived infancy. He was invested as Peter's heir when he was two years old. Not wishing to repeat the mistakes he had made with Alexei, Peter supervised Petrushka's education personally, instilling in him an early fondness for the same military games that had enlivened his own boyhood. Under Peter's tutelage, Petrushka learned to "[drill] soldiers and fire cannon" with aplomb. When he died on April 25, 1719, at the age of four, Peter and Catherine were crushed. They had weathered the deaths of nine of their children, but Petrushka had survived long enough to make them hope for the future.

The two children remaining to them were both daughters—Anna, born in 1708, and Elizaveta, born in 1709. Both girls were born illegitimate, but they were formally legitimized after Peter and Catherine married. Unlike Alexei, who had grown up in the old Russia and was already a man when Peter won his victory at Poltava, Anna and Elizaveta were princesses of the new Russia, and were raised to consider themselves the equals of the daughters of any monarchs in

Europe. Their educations would reflect this status. As an adult, Elizaveta would recollect the pains that their father had taken with their studies. She believed that Peter regretted abandoning his formal education; he often came to Elizaveta and Anna in their classroom to ask them what they had learned that day. Both of the girls were clever, particularly Anna, who had a scholarly bent, in comparison to Elizaveta's more pragmatic intelligence. Peter employed a French governess, who taught them to speak French, German, Spanish, and Swedish. An observer of the period remarked that, "[Anna] was a beautiful soul in a beautiful body…both in appearance and in manners, she was Peter's complete likeness, particularly in her character and mind … set off by her kind heart." Her younger sister Elizaveta, was no less beautiful; her nickname, when she was older, was "the Russian Venus".

One of Peter's greatest ambitions was to arrange a marriage between Elizaveta and Louis XV, who had succeeded his great-grandfather, Louis XIV, to the French throne when he was five years old. Elizaveta and he were the same age, and Elizaveta had been trained in the language, history, and courtly etiquette of France to prepare her for the marriage. If betrothal to the king was not an option, then some other high-born prince of the Bourbon house would do; once the marriage had taken place, Peter would install them, by force of arms if necessary, as king and queen of Poland. The French regent, Philippe d'Orleans, was interested in Peter's offer and even offered his own son as a potential bridegroom for Elizaveta, though this required him to overcome his distaste for the fact that Elizaveta's mother had been born a peasant. But the French wanted Peter to depose Augustus of Poland before the marriage took place, while Peter wanted the children to marry immediately; he would send them to Poland when Augustus died. Ultimately, interference from the English, who were now allies of the French and enemies of Russia, prevented the match from being made. But fate had a higher destiny in mind for Elizaveta, who would one day become empress of Russia.

Chapter Five: The Legacy of Peter the Great

Civil reform

In 1717, eight years after Poltava and eight years before his death, Peter had a conversation with Prince Jacob Dolgoruky, one of his oldest, most trusted advisors, a man upon whom Peter relied absolutely to speak the truth without fear of the tsar's anger. He asked him to consider the reign of his father, tsar Alexis, and compare it to his own reign. Prince Dolgoruky replied at length:

"A tsar has three main duties to perform. The most important is the administration of the country and the dispensation of justice. Your father had enough time to attend to this, while you have had none, which is why your father accomplished more than you. It is possible that when you do give some thought to this manner—

and it is time you did—you will do more than your father.

"A tsar's second duty is to the organization of the army. Here again, your father is to be praised because he laid the foundations of a regular army, thereby showing you the way. Unfortunately, certain misguided men undid all his work, so that you had to start all over again, and I must admit that you have done very well. Even so, I still do not know which of you has done better; we will only know when the war is over.

"And, finally, we come to a tsar's third duty, which is building a fleet, making treaties and determining our relationship with foreign countries. Here, and I hope you will agree with me, you have achieved more than your father. For this, you deserve much praise. Somebody tonight said that a tsar's work depends on his ministers. I disagree and think the opposite, since a wise monarch will choose wise counselors who know their worth. Therefore, a wise monarch will not tolerate stupid counselors because he will know their quality and be able to distinguish good advice from bad."

As a summary of Peter's reign to date, it was masterful. The war with Sweden had not ended in Poltava, though ultimately the power of the Swedish army had been broken there. Charles XII had fled into exile beyond the borders of the Ottoman empire, where he remained under the sultan's protection until 1710, when Peter invaded the Baltic peninsula in order to seize him. The Pruth campaign was a nearly unmitigated disaster for Peter, who was forced to cede Azov back to the Ottomans as part of his peace settlement with the sultan.

War had taken up nearly all of Peter's energy since he returned from his first journey west, and this was reflected in the administration of the Russian government. All power in Russia was concentrated in the hands of the autocrat; there were no legislators, independent or otherwise, with the authority to write or enact laws while the tsar's attention was occupied by other things. Thus far, Peter had governed by issuing edicts, usually in the form of scraps of paper on which he had scrawled a few sentences above his signature. He usually did not have the time to explain or discuss how his edicts were to be carried out, so this was left to his chief ministers, who often had their own agendas. A robust government has architects of policy who design broad-reaching laws that work together for the good of the country. Peter had no time to design such policies except as they pertained to building up the army, creating the navy, and drafting the necessary labor to build St. Petersburg.

All of this was about to change. The war with Sweden came to an effective end in 1718, when Charles XII was killed by a stray musket shot while inspecting trenches during his Norwegian campaign. This freed Peter to spend the last eight years of his life reforming the administration of his government. In 1711, before embarking on the Pruth river campaign, he had created the Senate, a legislative and administrative body to rule Russia in his absence. It had no power in itself, however, and the senators did not always take the job seriously. They were required to meet for three days a week, but not until Peter placed imperial guards in the senate room did the senators show up for work regularly. Even then, they were more inclined to drink and joke than attend to business. When they accomplished anything, it was usually due to the efforts of the First Senator, Jacob Dolgoruky, whose will was so strong and his devotion to the good of his country so great that he once dared Peter's ire by tearing up a decree he had issued, because he believed Peter had not thought it through carefully. When Peter demanded an explanation, Dolgoruky replied, "It is my zeal for your honor and the good of your subjects. Do not be angry,

Peter Alexeevich, that I have too much confidence in your wisdom to think you wish, like Charles XII, to desolate your country." Dolgoruky proceeded to explain his reason for opposing the edict, which had called for serfs to be requisitioned from St. Petersburg and Novgorod for the digging of the Ladoga Canal. These were the provinces that had been hit hardest by war requisitions; it made more sense to order serfs from other more populous provinces, and supplement their numbers with the labor of Swedish prisoners of war. Peter listened calmly, then ordered that everything be done as Dolgoruky had advised.

The Senate would have to be reformed if it was to be an effective arm of the government; Jacob Dolgoruky would not live forever, after all. Accordingly, Peter created the office of the Procurator General. He would not be a voting member of the Senate, but he would be its President, the tsar's eyes and ears on the council, who would relate Peter's wishes and oversee the Senate's efforts to carry them out. Furthermore, Peter came to recognize that the Senate had more work than it could handle, because it was responsible for both legislative and administrative duties. In the future, the Senate would be in charge of legislation only; the administration of the government was placed in the hands of "colleges", or ministries. There were nine of them: Foreign Affairs, Revenue Collection, Justice, Expenditure, Financial Control, War, Admiralty, Commerce, and Mining and Manufacturing. Each college would have a Russian president and a foreign vice-president. The college presidents would also serve as members of the Senate, effectively creating a cabinet of ministers. In a single stroke, Peter had modernized the Russian government, taking as his model the governments of England, Holland, and especially Sweden, where the government had continued to function seamlessly for fifteen years despite the fact that Charles XII had been fighting wars on foreign soil for most of his reign.

Peter's new government did not function smoothly right away. In most of his communications with the Senate, Peter took the tone of an angry parent or overtaxed schoolteacher, berating them for wasting time, gossiping, and failing to turn their assignments in on time. The governmental models he was attempting to emulate were not autocracies; to a certain extent, their monarchs were answerable to the people, and this made a considerable difference. An Englishman of high rank could be dismissed and disgraced for failing to execute the duties of his office, but he could not be summarily executed or exiled on the whim of the king. Peter's ministers, by contrast, were painfully aware that they could be sent to Siberia if they displeased him. Peter needed the people who ran his government to be self-motivated and independent, but as he gradually came to realize, it is impossible to *force* people to act independently. His ministers were naturally reluctant to assume responsibility when they knew that Peter was looking over their shoulder, waiting for them to make a wrong move.

After 1716, Peter altered his approach. He realized that it was necessary for officials at every level of government to understand the essential principles of governing before they could be expected to use their own judgment to make decisions. "Because I so order it," is the implicit reasoning that lies behind the decrees of all autocrats. Peter's new approach could be summarized as, "I so order it *because,*" followed by a thorough explanation of why a certain piece of legislation was needed, citing historical precedents and common sense arguments. Future tsars of Russia would follow this example, most famously Catherine the Great, who in 1767 convened a special assembly of representatives from across Russia, including all classes of society and all religious and ethnic groups, to perform a complete review and overhaul of the Russian legal code. Prior to convening the assembly, she spent two years writing a document called the *Nakaz,* or *Instructions to the Legislative Assembly,* which was nothing less than a master class in the theory of government, distilled in a few thousand words for the benefit of the people.

Probably the most unpopular of all Peter's civil reforms was the law that mandated a minimum of twenty-five years of state service for every able-bodied son of the nobility. Starting at the age of ten, boys from noble families were sent to schools where they were to complete five years of study in reading, writing, elementary arithmetic and geometry, after which they were awarded a certificate of completion. Unless a young man could produce one of these certificates, he was not allowed to marry. At the age of fifteen, boys were sent to the military or naval academies;

almost everyone preferred the military, and the classrooms of the naval academies had to be filled by conscription. Young men could also fulfill their service to the state by working for the civil service, but since this was considered the softer, safer option, Peter was forced to decree that only one son from each family could follow that route. This policy of mandatory state service was so unpopular that people often resorted to desperate measures to evade it, feigning illness, madness, or injury. Some became monks; others simply fled into the vast Russian countryside, where Peter's clerks could not find them. When Peter's grandson, Peter III, came to the throne, one of his first acts was to repeal the requirement for mandatory service, which made him very popular until he was deposed by Catherine the Great seven months later.

The Death of Peter the Great

Apart from the reformation of his government, the last few year of Peter's life were preoccupied by two principle questions: settling the succession, and arranging marriages for his young teenage daughters, Elizaveta and Anna. Negotiations with the French for Elizaveta's hand had failed, but she was the younger daughter; there would be time to dispose of her later. In the mean time, he began considering the suit of Charles Frederick, Duke of Holstein-Gottorp and nephew of Charles XII. Charles Frederick had arrived in Russia in 1721, three years after the death of Charles XII, hoping to persuade Peter to support his claim to the Swedish throne. Peter, who was negotiating a peace settlement with the Swedish government, was unwilling to become involved, but he made the young duke feel at home. Charles Frederick enjoyed great popularity in St. Petersburg. There were a number of Swedish officers who had become permanent exiles in Russia after the war, because they had married Russian wives, whom they were forbidden to bring home to Sweden. These young officers and their families gravitated to the Duke of Holstein, who became the glittering center of their social circle. After a few years, Charles Frederick renounced his claim on the Swedish throne, and was rewarded by Charles XII's successor with the title of Royal Highness and a pension. He was now eligible for marriage to the daughter of the Russian tsar, and the match with Anna was approved. Peter lived to see Anna's betrothal celebrations, but not her marriage, which took place a few weeks after his death.

When it came to the succession, Peter had limited options. With the death of his son Alexei in 1718, and the death of Petrushka in 1719, Peter himself represented the end of the male-descended Romanov line. He had once told Alexei that he would leave the throne of Russia to some worthy and well-qualified stranger rather than leave it to an unworthy member of his family. But the worthy person to whom his thoughts turned now was not a stranger; she was his wife. Catherine was not only the person closest to him, she was as much his equal as a Russian wife in the 18th century could be the equal of her husband. When Peter went to war with the sultan of the Ottoman empire, Catherine stood by his side on the front lines of the battle, demonstrating to the soldiers and the tsar alike that she was willing to share their danger. Her courage had not gone unnoticed by the Guards regiments, who adored her. Most importantly, Peter knew that she understood what he had been trying to achieve with his great reforms. Catherine's talents were not the same as his; she was unlikely to contribute much to the continuation of that work. But, crucially, Peter trusted her not to undermine it.

In February of 1722, Peter issued an *ukase*, or decree, stating that male primogeniture was a dangerous practice, unfounded in Scripture, that encouraged "the sin of Absalom", i.e. rebellion of a son and heir against his king and father. No one had to wonder who Peter was thinking of when he referenced the Biblical story of King David's rebellious son, who had hanged himself to evade his father's retribution. From now on—or at least, until his great-grandson Paul I overturned his edict some sixty years later—every tsar would be free to name whomsoever he wished as his successor.

This decree, like so many of Peter's decrees, came as a profound shock to traditional Muscovites. But in November of 1723, he shocked them even further. Peter had been declared emperor after the Treaty of Nystad brought a formal end to the war with Sweden in August of 1721. The Russian Senate had rewarded Peter for this victory by declaring him, "Peter the Great, Emperor of All Russia". At the same time, Catherine had received the conjugal title of empress, but now Peter determined to make the title more than a courtesy. Catherine would be, not only his wife, but his co-sovereign. Just as his hero, William of Orange, had ruled England with his wife Queen Mary, Peter would rule Russia with his wife, Empress Catherine.

The formal decree read:

"[Whereas] our best beloved Spouse, Consort and Empress Catherine has been a great support to us, and not only in this, but also in many military operations, putting aside womanly weakness, of her own will she has been present with us and has helped in every way possible... for these labors of our Spouse we have decided that by virtue of the supreme power given to us by God, she shall be crowned, which, God willing, is to take place formally in Moscow in the present winter."

The *ukase* made no mention of the succession, but Peter made a point of letting it be quietly known amongst high churchmen and members of the Senate that he was crowning Catherine as his co-ruler so that she would be in position to step smoothly into his place when he died. This was a stunning act: no tsarina had ever shared the burden of the monarchy with her husband, and no woman had ever ruled Russia in her own right. William and Mary had established a European precedent, but Mary was the daughter of King James II; Catherine was a Lithuanian peasant girl, a former servant and prisoner of war who had been Peter's mistress, and possibly the mistress of Menshikov. Her father's name was not even known.

From a historical point of view, however, Peter's decision is in keeping with his lifelong custom of promoting and elevating people based on merit, rather than birth and precedence. If he could overlook Menshikov's low birth to make him the second most powerful man in Russia, it is hardly surprising that he could overlook Catherine's sex to make her Empress. Besides, Peter had seen first hand that a woman could rule Russia. Though he feared and mistrusted his sister Sophia, he had never accused her of being anything less than supremely intelligent and capable.

In 1722, Peter began to experience the first symptoms of strangury, the illness that would eventually claim his life. Blockages were forming in his urethra which prevented him from expressing urine from his bladder. Off and on for the next three years, it would cause him to suffer bouts of extreme pain, fever, bloating, and other signs of infection. Then it would pass, and he would be well again. On his doctors' recommendation, Peter altered his lifestyle, drinking a great less than he had in his youth, and "taking the waters" at mineral spas in Germany and Russia, which in the eighteenth century was a commonly prescribed remedy for all manner of complaints. The list of foods which his doctors forbade him to eat during his illnesses included raw fruit, cucumber, lemons with salt, and Limburger cheese. He did not always abide strictly by this prescription—he is recorded as having eaten four pounds of cherries and figs during one of his bouts of illness—but a modern doctor would probably admit that it made little difference.

In 1724, Peter's suffering was so extreme that doctors were forced to insert a catheter in his urethra, a gruesome medical procedure when undergone without anesthesia. A doctor stood on either side of him, gripping his hands as the catheter forced an opening for the removal of a huge stone. Peter neither screamed nor cried, but he nearly broke the hands of the doctors. The procedure provided him with relief for about half a year. Then, shortly after the New Year in January of 1725, he came down with a high fever and became so delirious that he was forced to take to his bed. An examination by half a dozen panicked doctors revealed an infection so far advanced that gangrene had formed in his bladder. Frantically, they consulted with every European medical expert available in St. Petersburg and all that could be reached by special courier. But there was nothing to be done.

For about three weeks, he was well enough to conduct business from his bed. Then, on January 23, he became so ill that he called for Last Rites to be administered. As an act of deathbed clemency, he ordered the release of every prison being held by the state for any charge less severe than murder, and granted amnesty to young noblemen who had been arrested for attempting to evade their mandatory government service. Calling his foreign minister to his bedside, he made him swear to safeguard the foreigners who had come to live in Russia at his urging. Then, on the 26th, he began to suffer convulsions. All the ministers in his service were called to the palace to await the end. Painfully aware that he was on the verge of being called to answer to God for all that he had done in a long career that included prosecuting wars and torturing prisoners, he asked for Last Rites to be administered again. "I hope God will forgive me my many sins because of the good I have tried to do for my people," he murmured after.

Empress Catherine remained next to Peter's bedside throughout, holding his hand and soothing him as best she could as he lay wracked by intense pain and delirium. By then, he was incapable of speech. But he was still conscious, and the succession seems to have been weighing on his mind. Three days before he died, he asked for pen and paper to be brought to him, on which scrawled the words, "Give all to…" Then his hand fell from the paper, lacking strength to continue writing. He then asked for his daughter, Anna, presumably so she could write while he dictated, though some historians have speculated that he may have intended to name her as his successor. But by the time she arrived, he was too delirious to speak. Shortly afterwards, he fell into a coma, from which he never awakened.

One historian describes Peter the Great's final moments thus:

> "At last, at six o'clock in the morning of January 28, 1725, just as [Catherine] was pleading, 'O Lord, I pray Thee, open Thy paradise to receive unto Thyself this great soul,' Peter the Great, in the fifty-third year of his life and the forty-third year of his reign, entered eternity."

The legacy of Peter the Great

Catherine was acclaimed empress shortly after Peter's death; no one protested the decision. Menshikov, and a number of other ministers who, like him, had been appointed by Peter to high office despite their low birth, were keenly aware that if the succession went to anyone else, they would shortly be out of power. It was Menshikov who summoned Peter's Imperial Guards to the palace and reminded him that they had seen Catherine suffer danger and hardship alongside them during the war against the sultan. Like the Streltsy of old, the Guards were now the ultimate arbiters of imperial successions. They immediately declared for Catherine, crying, "Our father is dead, but our mother still lives." No one dared oppose them.

Peter's body lay in state so that the public could pay their respects for over a month. In early March, it was taken to the unfinished Peter and Paul Cathedral; it was not interred until construction was completed in 1731. Peter and Catherine's seven-year-old daughter, Natalia Petrovna, died of measles on March 25. Her small coffin was placed next to her father's.

Catherine was forty-two years old when she was acclaimed Empress. True to Peter's hopes, she acted as the guardian of his reforms, taking special care to cultivate the trust of the army, who were always paid punctually. Menshikov remained her closest advisor, and the de facto head of the government. Her reign lasted for only two years before she died in 1727, succeeded by the eleven-year-old Peter Alexeevich, son of the ill-fated tsarevitch Alexei. Her daughters, Anna and Elizaveta, were named to the Privy Council to help act as his regents.

A few weeks after Peter's death, Anna was married to Duke Charles Frederick, after which she returned with him to live in Holstein. The match would not prove a happy one. Out from under the watchful eye of Anna's family, especially her titan of a father, Charles Frederick proved a neglectful, unfaithful husband. Anna wrote often to Elizaveta, expressing her misery. She died four years later, at the age of twenty, from childbed fever, following the birth of her son.

In 1727, Elizaveta was betrothed to Charles Augustus of Holstein-Gottorp, first cousin of Anna's husband Charles Frederick. She was extremely attached to him, but two weeks before the wedding was to take place, he contracted smallpox and died a short time later, probably as a result of repeated bloodlettings. The blow fell all the heavier, because her mother, Empress Catherine, had died on two weeks before that. Now that she was no longer the daughter of a reigning monarch, there was very little chance she would ever marry again—although her nephew, Peter II, was extremely attached to her, and probably would have married her had he survived to adulthood. There was talk of Elizaveta becoming empress after Peter II's death, but he was succeeded instead by her first cousin, Anna of Courland, daughter of tsar Ivan and his wife Praskovia. Anna, who was jealous and suspicious of Peter the Great's daughter, chose not to make Elizaveta her heir, instead leaving the throne to Ivan, the infant son of her niece, also named Anna, who acted as his regent for six months. Elizaveta, backed by her father's Preobrazhensky Guards, staged a coup to remove Anna and Ivan from the palace. In December of 1741, she was acclaimed Empress Elizabeth I.

Since Elizabeth had no children of her own, she adopted the fourteen-year-old son of her beloved sister Anna and brought him to Russia to raise him as her heir. This was Karl Peter Ulrich, the Duke of Holstein, grandson of both Peter the Great and Charles XII, heir to the throne Sweden. Shortly after he arrived in Russia,

Elizabeth began searching for a suitable bride. She turned to Johanna von Anhalt-Zerbst, the sister of her deceased fiancé Charles Augustus, whose fourteen-year-old daughter was the cousin of the newly created Grand Duke Peter. This was Sophie Fredericke Auguste, who, after her conversion to the Orthodox faith, became known as Catherine. Elizabeth chose the name for her, in memory of mother, the Empress Catherine.

Six months after the Empress Elizabeth's death, Catherine deposed her husband, Peter III, and became sovereign empress of Russia. She saw herself as a reformer, a modernizer and westernizer of Russia, whose destiny it was to take up the mantle of Peter the Great and continue in his footsteps. Near the end of her reign, she commissioned a bronze statue of Peter on horseback, to emphasize her connection with his legacy. It is inscribed, in Russian and Latin, "To Peter I, from Catherine II."

Other great books by Michael W. Simmons on Kindle, paperback and audio:

Elizabeth I: Legendary Queen Of England

Alexander Hamilton: First Architect Of The American Government

William Shakespeare: An Intimate Look Into The Life Of The Most Brilliant Writer In The History Of The English Language

Thomas Edison: American Inventor

Catherine the Great: Last Empress of Russia

Romanov: The Last Tsarist Dynasty

Further Reading

Peter the Great, by Robert K. Massie

The Romanovs, by Simon Sebag Montefiore

The History of Peter the Great, by Voltaire

> https://archive.org/stream/historyofpetergr00volt/historyofpetergr00volt_djvu.txt

The History of Charles XII, King of Sweden, by Voltaire

> https://archive.org/stream/voltaireshistory00voltuoft/voltaireshistory00voltuoft_djvu.txt

Samuel Collins on the Court of Alexei Mikhailovich

> http://academic.shu.edu/russianhistory/index.php/Samuel_Collins,_On_the_Present_State_of_Russia

Excerpts from the writings of Johann-Georg Kerb from the court of Peter the Great

http://sourcebooks.fordham.edu/mod/petergreat.asp

Made in the USA
Middletown, DE
13 January 2018